I0626921

The Human User Manual

Unlock Your Potential, Master Your Mind, and
Transform Your Life

by

ROBERT G. ELLIS

Table of Contents

Introduction

Welcome to *The Human User Manual*—your ultimate guide to mastering the most powerful system you will ever operate: **yourself**. You are a remarkable being with infinite potential, yet, like any intricate tool, unlocking your capabilities requires understanding, practice, and intention. This book is your blueprint for building mental clarity, emotional resilience, and purposeful action. Through practical techniques, timeless wisdom, and transformative strategies, you'll gain the knowledge to not just survive but thrive. By the end of this journey, you will be equipped to take full control of your mind, emotions, and destiny.

This is not a book of abstract theories or untested ideas. Instead, it's built on real-world experience and lessons learned from life itself. While I am not a psychologist, the tools and principles I share come from years of personal exploration, the teachings of remarkable mentors, and, most importantly, the wisdom gained through my own mistakes. Life has been my greatest teacher, and it can be yours too—if you learn to observe yourself with compassion rather than judgment.

As the timeless saying goes, "Man, know thyself." This knowledge is the foundation of transformation. Once you truly understand yourself, external circumstances lose their power to control you. Stress reactions are replaced with calm resilience, and life becomes a reflection of your inner peace. But let me be clear: **results are always the byproduct of action.** The principles in this book can improve your life, but only if you put them into practice. Without action, no meaningful transformation can occur, and the responsibility for inaction rests with you.

At the core of this book are two foundational tools: **positive affirmations** and **meditation**. These are not merely "feel-good" practices but proven techniques for reprogramming the subconscious mind and fostering lasting improvements. Affirmations replace negative thought patterns with empowering beliefs, while meditation anchors these affirmations into your consciousness, creating a ripple effect of peace, clarity, and focus. When practiced consistently, these techniques can reduce or even eliminate stress, empowering you to face life's challenges with grace and composure.

Why Practice Matters

We've all heard the phrase "Practice makes perfect," and yet many of us fall short when it comes to applying this wisdom to self-improvement. Imagine reading a book about playing tennis and then stepping onto the court for the first time, expecting to excel. Without practice, your initial attempts would likely be clumsy. But with persistence, day after day, you would improve until eventually, you'd master the game. The same is true for mastering your mind.

Take the example of a baby learning to walk. They stumble, fall, and try again countless times before finally succeeding. Failure isn't a deterrent—it's simply part of the process. Imagine if babies gave up after their first few falls, afraid of failure or embarrassment. If that were the case, many adults would still be crawling on their hands and knees, held back by fear. However, a baby's intention to walk is so strong that it never gives up. The instinct to persevere—until walking becomes second nature—is something we are all born with. This natural drive for growth and success still resides within you; it simply needs to be reawakened.

How to Practice Positive Affirmations

Positive affirmations are one of the cornerstone techniques for reprogramming your subconscious mind. Each chapter in this book provides carefully crafted affirmations designed to help you reduce stress, build resilience, and master your inner world. To maximize their effectiveness:

1. **Commit to 21 Days**: Consistent repetition is key. Practice each set of affirmations daily for at least 21 days to establish lasting habits.

2. **Speak with Intention**: Say each affirmation slowly and with conviction, allowing the words to resonate deeply within you.

3. **Visualize Success**: As you say the affirmations, imagine yourself embodying their energy and achieving the outcomes they describe, as if it

already is so.

4. **Meditate with Affirmations**: Spend a few minutes in meditation after practicing your affirmations, letting their meaning settle into your consciousness.

5. **Reflect on Progress**: Keep a journal to track how your mindset and reactions evolve over time.

6. **Create a Safe Space**: Practice in a quiet, comfortable environment where you can focus without distractions.

When paired with meditation, affirmations become more than words—they become a pathway to transformation. Over time, you'll notice subtle yet profound shifts in your mindset, leading to a calmer, more focused, and more empowered version of yourself.

Super Charge Your Practice

Combining goals, meditation, affirmations, and visualizations creates a transformative synergy that can supercharge positive change in your life. Goals provide the direction—a clear destination that fuels your motivation and focus. Meditation calms the mind, creating a receptive state where affirmations and visualizations can take root more deeply. Affirmations rewire your subconscious, replacing self-doubt with empowering beliefs. Visualization bridges the gap between intention and reality, engaging your senses and emotions to make your aspirations feel tangible and attainable. Together, these practices align your thoughts, emotions, and actions, creating a powerful framework for lasting growth and success. This holistic approach not only amplifies your progress but also fosters a sense of inner peace, resilience, and purpose.

The Importance of Taking Action

Ultimately, this book is a guide, not a magic wand. I can show you the path, but I cannot walk it for you. The power to improve your life lies within you, and it begins with a single step: **action.** Without action, inspiration is fleeting, and knowledge remains dormant.

The techniques I share have worked for me, and they can work for you too—but only if you use them. Experiment, observe, and apply these tools with consistency. As you do, you'll notice real, tangible improvements: reduced stress, greater clarity, a calmer mind, and a deeper sense of purpose.

Let this book be your companion on the journey to becoming your best self. Embrace the teachings, commit to the practices, and watch as your life transforms in ways you never thought possible.

As an aside, I've spent decades as a software engineer across various industries, and I've drawn on that experience to create an app to support mindfulness and meditation practices. It's called *UMeditate*. This app enhances the practices outlined in this book by providing mindfulness alerts and timed meditations, complete with Tibetan bells to mark the beginning and end of your sessions.

The app offers free access to its basic features for life, with optional subscriptions for advanced functionalities. However, the tools and insights shared in this book are entirely effective on their own. *UMeditate* is simply an optional resource to deepen your experience, should you choose to use it. Whether or not you decide to try the app, you'll find everything you need within these pages to embark on your journey of mindfulness and transformation.

At the time of this edition's release, *UMeditate* is available exclusively for iOS, with an Android version planned for the future.

Here is the link in case you want to check it out:

https://apps.apple.com/us/app/umeditate/id6450525722

Now let's get started. Your best life is waiting. Take the first step—and then another, and another—until success becomes your new reality.

The Power of Goals

This book is not about goal setting. However, having goals is incredibly important because they serve as the foundation for applying the techniques taught in this book. When you know what you want to achieve or where you intend to go, it adds fuel to your transformative journey. Goals act as the rocket fuel that helps you blast off and keep going, especially when challenges arise. You'll be amazed at how much more effective these transformative techniques become when you have a clear destination in mind.

That said, even if you don't currently have any specific goals, the techniques in this book will still be very helpful. They are designed to foster self-awareness, resilience, and personal transformation in ways that can benefit anyone, regardless of their starting point. However, having goals in mind provides a compass for your efforts, making the impact of these techniques noticeably more powerful. Goals help you channel your energy and focus on meaningful outcomes, amplifying the results of your practice.

If you're unsure about your goals right now, don't worry—this book will still guide you toward positive improvement. And as you move forward, you may find that goals naturally emerge as your understanding and perspective expand.

Why Goals Matter

Imagine stepping into a car without knowing where you're going. You could drive aimlessly, wasting fuel and time, and still not arrive anywhere meaningful. Goals act as the destination on your map, giving you clarity, purpose, and a sense of direction. They help you navigate challenges and ensure your efforts are aligned with your vision for the future.

Without goals, life becomes random and reactive. Like a ship drifting on the ocean without a set destination, you may float aimlessly, but the tides and winds will ultimately determine your fate. Such a ship might crash into rocks or reach an undesirable destination. In contrast, having clear goals allows you to steer your life with purpose, making intentional choices that lead to the outcomes you truly desire.

What If You Don't Know What You Want?

If you're unsure about what you want to achieve, don't let that hold you back. Make something up. Often, the act of choosing a goal—any goal—creates the clarity and momentum you need to discover your true desires. Think back to your childhood dreams. What fascinated you? What filled you with excitement and curiosity? Childhood desires can serve as a great starting point for setting goals, even if they seem impractical or unrelated to your current life.

For example, when I was a child, I always dreamed of learning to fly. Many decades ago, I found myself in a similar situation where I had no clear goals. I was reading a book on goal setting, and the author recommended choosing a goal, even if it felt made up. So, I decided my goal would be to earn my pilot's license within two years.

To my amazement, because I followed through with action, I achieved that goal. I didn't stop there. My next goal was to own my own airplane, which I accomplished. Eventually, I upgraded from a single-engine airplane to a twin-engine airplane. All of this started from making up a goal when I didn't know what I wanted.

The act of pursuing and achieving those goals taught me valuable lessons about discipline, focus, and the joy of progress. Even if your initial goals seem arbitrary, the process of working toward them can unlock new aspirations and set you on a path toward greater fulfillment.

State Your Goals in the Positive

Goals should be stated in the positive and follow the following guidelines:
- **Clear and Specific**: Be precise about your goals. The more specific, the better.
- **Positive and Empowering**: Focus on what you desire, not what you fear or wish to avoid.
- **Actionable**: Include steps that guide you toward your goal.

Furthermore, one of the most important principles of goal setting is that your goals should be supported by clear, meaningful reasons why they matter to you. These reasons must be stated in the positive, as the subconscious mind is incapable of processing negativity. To the subconscious, everything simply is. For example, when you say, "I don't want to be poor," your subconscious interprets it as "I be poor," because it focuses on the dominant idea—poverty. This is why people who frame their goals negatively often fail to achieve success; their focus remains on what they want to avoid, rather than what they want to create. And the fact is that we tend to achieve what we focus on the most. In the above example, the person focusing on negative reasons for their goal ends up drawing the negative outcome into their reality—the very thing they desperately wish to avoid. Instead, they need to be focusing on the positive—the thing they want to achieve.

For example:

- Instead of **"I don't want to feel overwhelmed,"** say, **"I manage my responsibilities with clarity and confidence."**
- Instead of **"I don't want to feel tired all the time,"** say, **"I prioritize rest and energy-boosting habits to feel refreshed and energized daily."**
- Instead of **"I don't want to be unhealthy,"** say, **"I embrace a lifestyle of health and vitality through balanced nutrition and regular exercise."**
- Instead of **"I don't want to be broke,"** say, **"I create financial stability by managing my resources wisely and pursuing opportunities for growth."**
- Instead of **"I don't want to be lonely,"** say, **"I build meaningful relationships by connecting authentically with others."**

These examples focus on what you aim to create rather than what you want to avoid, encouraging proactive and goal-oriented thinking.

Positive goals backed by positive descriptions not only align with your subconscious mind but also create a sense of excitement and possibility that propels you forward.

The Spiritual Aspect of Goal Achievement

For those of you who are spiritually oriented, achieving your goals isn't just about material or personal success—it's a profound step forward in the expansion of consciousness. When you go from where you are to accomplishing something meaningful, you grow in experience, understanding, and awareness. Every step you take toward a goal broadens your perspective and strengthens your connection to your higher potential.

This growth aligns with a deeper universal truth: we are here to evolve, to expand our understanding of what is possible, and to contribute positively to the world. By setting and achieving goals, you participate in this grand journey of consciousness expansion, both individually and collectively.

Practical Steps for Goal Setting

If you already have goals in mind, here's how to refine them:
1. **Write Them Down**: Putting your goals in writing makes them real and tangible.
2. **State Them Positively**: Frame them in terms of what you want, not what you want to avoid.
3. **Visualize Success**: Picture yourself achieving your goals and experiencing the rewards of your efforts.
4. **Break Them Into Steps**: Divide big goals into smaller, actionable steps to maintain progress.
5. **Celebrate Wins**: Acknowledge milestones to stay motivated.

If you're unsure about your goals, start small. Experiment with simple, achievable goals, and allow the process to reveal new possibilities. Even a seemingly modest goal can lead to profound improvements in your life.

If you're not sure how to set goals, don't worry—this book isn't meant to be a comprehensive guide on goal setting. There are plenty of excellent books dedicated to the topic. I encourage you to find one that resonates with you and use it alongside this book. When paired with clear, positive goals, the techniques taught here will help you achieve transformation faster and more effectively than you might expect.

Transform with Intention

While this book provides the tools for transformation, the power to steer your life comes from setting clear and positive goals. Having a destination in mind amplifies the impact of these techniques, giving you the motivation and clarity to push forward. Whether your goal is personal growth, financial freedom, or improved relationships, let it guide your journey and keep you on course.

Delays in reaching your goals do not signify failure. Think of an airliner encountering unexpected bad weather. If the weather delays its arrival, is that a failure? Of course not. The pilot doesn't abandon the journey or give up; they adjust course, navigate through the turbulence, and continue toward the destination. Similarly, unforeseen circumstances or miscalculations in how long it might take to achieve your goals are not failures—they are simply delays. The key is to remain committed and persistent. Be gentle and loving with yourself when setbacks occur. Adjust your timeline if needed, and remember that the journey is still moving forward, even if progress feels slower than expected.

Take a moment now to reflect on your aspirations. Where do you want to go? What do you want to achieve? Write it down and hold that vision in your mind. Then, as you apply the practices in this book, watch as your goals come to life, one step at a time.

Meditation

Meditation is a powerful tool that enhances the effectiveness of the affirmations and techniques in this book. While affirmations can be transformative on their own, using them during meditation elevates their impact. Meditation creates a state of deep relaxation and focused attention, allowing affirmations to penetrate the subconscious mind more effectively. This combination accelerates the process of reprogramming your mind and fostering transformation.

Meditation doesn't have to be complicated or time-consuming. At its core, it's about focusing your attention and calming your mind. Anyone can meditate, regardless of experience, and the practice can be adapted to suit your preferences. Whether you meditate with your eyes open or closed, it's essential to choose the approach that feels right for you. Most people prefer closing their eyes to block out distractions and focus inward, while others find keeping their eyes open helps them stay alert. Experiment to find what works best.

Personally, I prefer to meditate with my eyes closed. Closing my eyes helps me shut out visual distractions and focus more deeply on my inner world. I also meditate every day in the same spot in my house. There's an esoteric reason for this, but I will not expand on that here. What's most important is finding a method and environment that feels comfortable and supportive for you.

It is important to note that meditation should never be practiced while driving, operating machinery, or engaging in any activity requiring full concentration. Safety must always come first. Meditation is best done in a quiet and relaxed setting where you can focus without interruption. However, it can also be done while commuting by bus or train, as long as the environment allows for focus without excessive distraction.

Getting Started with Meditation

To begin meditating, find a quiet space where you won't be disturbed. It doesn't need to be completely silent, but fewer distractions will help you focus. Sit comfortably, either on a chair with your feet flat on the floor or on a cushion with your legs crossed. The key is to find a position that is both relaxed and alert, with your back straight but not stiff. A comfortable posture helps you stay focused without unnecessary tension.

Once seated, take a few deep breaths to settle your mind. Let your breathing return to its natural rhythm and bring your attention to the sensation of your breath. Notice how it feels as it enters your nose, fills your lungs, and then gently leaves your body. With each exhalation, allow yourself to go deeper and deeper into relaxation, releasing tension from every muscle, tendon, and ligament in your body, from head to toe. You can also focus on relaxing one section of your body at a time. For example, start with your head and face, then move to your neck and shoulders, arms and hands, torso and internal organs, upper legs, lower legs, and finally your feet. Alternatively, you can imagine scanning your body from head to toe like a laser copier, relaxing each part of your body as the imaginary laser passes over it with each exhalation. Experiment with these techniques to find what works best for you. This simple practice of focusing on your breath and body can calm your thoughts and help bring you fully into the present moment.

When you feel centered, introduce an affirmation. For example, you might repeat silently or softly aloud, "I am calm, confident, and in control of my life." Focus on the meaning of the words, allowing them to resonate deeply. If your mind starts to wander, gently bring your attention back to the affirmation or your breath. Wandering thoughts are natural—use them as opportunities to practice returning to the present.

When you're ready to end your meditation, take a few deep breaths and slowly bring your awareness back to your surroundings. Open your eyes if they were closed, stretch if needed, and take a moment to transition back into your day.

Enhancing Affirmations Through Meditation

Pairing affirmations with meditation creates a powerful synergy. Meditation quiets the mental noise and makes your mind more receptive to affirmations. This allows positive statements to sink deeply into your subconscious, where they can start to rewire your beliefs and behaviors. For example, if you are focusing on building confidence, repeating "I am worthy of success and happiness" during meditation reinforces your sense of self-worth. If reducing stress is your goal, meditating with the affirmation "I am calm and at peace" creates a profound sense of relaxation and stability. These affirmations, combined with the meditative state, become more effective in shaping your inner reality.

Consistency Over Perfection

Like any new skill, meditation improves with practice. You don't need to spend hours meditating every day to see results; even five minutes a day can make a difference. Start small and gradually increase the time as you become more comfortable. Consistency is key. Meditating regularly, even for short periods, can lead to noticeable improvements in focus, resilience, and emotional well-being.

Creating a routine can help establish meditation as a habit. Meditating at the same time and place each day can make the practice more impactful. Personally, I've found that meditating in the same spot daily strengthens my focus and helps create a sense of familiarity and ease. While I won't delve into the esoteric reasons behind this, I encourage you to try it and see how it works for you.

Be patient with yourself. Meditation isn't about forcing your mind to be empty—it's about gently guiding your focus, relaxing your body, calming your emotions, and bringing your attention back when it drifts. It's a journey, not a destination. So keep practicing, and with time, you'll find yourself growing stronger, calmer, and more centered with every step forward.

Why Meditation Matters

Meditation not only enhances the effectiveness of affirmations but also offers numerous other benefits. It reduces stress and anxiety, improves focus and clarity, increases emotional resilience, and fosters a sense of inner peace. By incorporating meditation into your routine, you create a foundation of mindfulness and self-awareness that supports every aspect of your transformation.

Even if you don't meditate daily, practicing a few times a week can significantly enhance your ability to absorb the techniques in this book. Meditation helps you tap into your inner resources and align your conscious and subconscious mind with your goals, making it a valuable tool for personal growth.

Closing Thoughts

Meditation is a simple yet transformative practice that complements everything you'll learn in this book. Whether you meditate for five minutes or an hour, the time you spend connecting with your inner self is invaluable. Use the guidance in this chapter to get started, and don't worry about perfection. The most important step is to begin, because results are a by-product of action.

Pair your affirmations with meditation to supercharge their impact, and watch as your subconscious mind shifts to align with the life you want to create. By dedicating even a small amount of time to this practice, you open the door to profound transformation and lasting improvements.

Visualization: Unlock the Life You Intend To Achieve

Visualization is one of the most powerful tools available to you for creating the life you desire. It is a process that bridges the gap between your current reality and the future you want to manifest. At its core, visualization is the practice of using your imagination to vividly picture your goals and desires as though they are already achieved. It is not merely an exercise in daydreaming or wishful thinking—visualization is a focused, intentional act of aligning your mind, emotions, and actions with a specific outcome.

Here's the truth: everyone is already visualizing, whether they realize it or not. Most people, however, unknowingly visualize negative outcomes. They imagine worst-case scenarios, replay fears, and focus on potential failures. And what happens? Their lives often reflect these negative mental images, reinforcing a cycle of worry and dissatisfaction.

If your life doesn't feel like it reflects the positive, fulfilling reality you desire, it's time to examine what you've been visualizing. Pay attention to your thoughts and inner dialogue. Are you frequently imagining setbacks, struggles, or limitations? If so, these mental patterns may be holding you back. The good news is that you have the power to change this. By becoming aware of your visualizations and intentionally shifting them toward positive outcomes, you can redirect the course of your life.

When you visualize with clarity and emotional intensity, you create a mental blueprint of your goals. This mental image acts as a compass, directing your subconscious mind toward the actions and opportunities necessary to bring your vision to life. Visualization not only strengthens your belief in what is possible but also ignites the motivation and determination needed to pursue your goals relentlessly.

What makes visualization so effective is its ability to engage your senses and emotions. By vividly imagining the sights, sounds, feelings, and even smells associated with achieving your goal, you create a mental experience that feels real to your brain. This activates the same neural pathways that would fire if you were actually living the experience, training your brain to perceive your goal as attainable and familiar.

Unlike passive daydreaming, effective visualization requires focus and intention. It invites you to take an active role in shaping your reality by clarifying what you want, immersing yourself in the feeling of having already achieved it, and using that energy to inspire action. It's a practice rooted in the principle that your thoughts create your reality—what you focus on expands.

Visualization is not limited to grand, life-changing goals. It can be used to enhance any area of your life, from career ambitions and personal relationships to health, fitness, and financial success. No matter the size or scope of your goal, visualization allows you to rehearse success in your mind, preparing you to act with confidence and purpose in the real world.

By practicing visualization regularly and focusing on positive, empowering outcomes, you harness the immense power of your mind to shape your destiny. It aligns your inner world with your outer actions, paving the way for transformation and fulfillment. Visualization is the ultimate tool for transforming intention into reality, turning dreams into achievable milestones, and creating a life that reflects your highest aspirations. If you've been visualizing negativity, change the narrative. Start today, and watch how the power of positive visualization transforms your life.

The Science Behind Visualization

Your mind cannot distinguish between vividly imagined experiences and real ones. This remarkable aspect of the brain is a cornerstone of visualization's transformative power. When you visualize with clarity and emotion, your brain activates the same neural pathways as it would if you were actually experiencing the event. This creates a kind of mental rehearsal, effectively "programming" your mind to act as though the visualized outcome is already your reality.

This phenomenon isn't just theory—it's backed by science. Studies in neuroscience reveal that the brain doesn't differentiate between real and imagined stimuli. When you vividly imagine achieving a goal—seeing yourself on stage delivering a powerful speech, crossing the finish line of a marathon, or closing a major deal—your brain fires the same neurons as it would if you were actually living those moments. Over time, these mental rehearsals strengthen neural connections, building new pathways that prime your mind for success.

This is why elite athletes, successful entrepreneurs, and top performers across industries swear by the practice of visualization. For athletes, visualizing a perfect performance can improve muscle memory and boost confidence. They imagine every detail of their success: the sound of the crowd, the feel of the equipment, the rush of adrenaline, and the joy of victory. Their brains become so familiar with the desired outcome that when they step onto the field, court, or track, their bodies instinctively follow the "script" they've mentally rehearsed.

The same applies to entrepreneurs and business leaders. Visualization helps them prepare for critical meetings, navigate challenges, and confidently execute their vision. By mentally rehearsing success, they reduce uncertainty and anxiety, replacing them with focus and determination. Visualization becomes a tool not just for planning but for embodying the qualities and behaviors necessary for achieving their goals.

The beauty of this practice is that it's accessible to everyone, not just high achievers. You can apply visualization to any area of your life—whether it's landing a new job, improving your relationships, or achieving personal health goals. By vividly imagining the steps you'll take, the obstacles you'll overcome, and the emotions you'll feel when you succeed, you're essentially training your mind to believe that your goal is not only possible but inevitable.

It's important to note that effective visualization goes beyond just imagining the end result. The most impactful visualizations also focus on the process—the small, consistent actions that lead to success. For example, if your goal is to run a marathon, don't just picture yourself crossing the finish line. Imagine the training runs, the discipline to wake up early, and the feeling of pushing through fatigue. By visualizing both the journey and the destination, you prepare your mind to embrace the challenges and persevere.

Ultimately, visualization is more than a mental exercise—it's a bridge between intention and action. When you combine the mental clarity of visualization with focused effort in the real world, you unlock the potential to create a reality that aligns with your vision. The more vividly and consistently you visualize success, the more your brain will guide your actions to make it a tangible outcome.

How to Practice Visualization

Set a Clear Intention: Before you begin, decide on a specific goal or outcome you want to achieve. The clearer your vision, the more powerful your visualization will be.

Create a Relaxed Environment: Find a quiet space where you won't be disturbed. Sit comfortably, close your eyes, and take a few deep breaths to relax your body and calm your mind.

After achieving a calm relaxed meditative state, continue with the following:

Engage All Your Senses: In your mind's eye, vividly imagine your goal as though it's already achieved. Picture yourself in the scene—what do you see, hear, feel, smell, and even taste? The more sensory details you include, the more real your visualization becomes.

Feel the Emotion: Imagine the joy, pride, gratitude, or excitement you would feel upon achieving your goal. Emotions amplify the impact of visualization and make it resonate more deeply with your subconscious mind.

Repeat Consistently: Make visualization a daily habit. Spend a few minutes every morning or before bed focusing on your vision. Consistency is key to reinforcing the mental pathways that lead to success.

Visualization in Action

When I first decided to earn my pilot's license, I had no idea how I would achieve it. But every day, I visualized myself flying a plane. I imagined the controls in my hands, the wind beneath the wings, and the exhilarating feeling of freedom as I soared through the sky.

After earning my pilot's license, I set my sights on owning my own airplane. At the time, I didn't have the income to afford one. But I refused to let that stop me. Every night before going to sleep, I entered a meditative state and visualized myself shaking the hand of a seller, handing him a box of money, and receiving the keys to my very own airplane. I repeated this visualization every night until it became a deeply ingrained reality in my mind.

To reinforce my vision, I surrounded myself with reminders of my goal. I hung photos of the airplane I wanted on my refrigerator so I would see it every day. I set the background image on my computer to that same airplane, ensuring the outcome I desired remained constantly in my awareness. These visual cues kept me focused and motivated.

Not long after, I found a much better-paying job that gave me the income I needed to make my dream a reality. I was able to buy a single-engine airplane. Over time, what started as a mental image became my real-life experience. That visualization not only fueled my determination but also inspired me to take the necessary steps to achieve my goal.

Using the same technique, within two years, I leveled up to a twin-engine airplane. Visualization was the bridge between my dreams and reality, and it taught me that aligning your mind with your goals can make even the most ambitious dreams possible.

You can apply this technique to achieve any goal you set for yourself—whether it's related to finances, health, career, relationships, or any other area of your life. Keep this in mind as you progress through each chapter of this book.

Overcoming Common Challenges

Doubt and Fear: If you find it hard to believe in your visualization, start with smaller, more achievable goals. Success breeds confidence, and confidence amplifies your ability to visualize effectively.

Distractions: If your mind wanders, gently bring it back to the scene you're imagining. Over time, your focus will improve.

Lack of Clarity: If your vision feels fuzzy, spend time journaling about your goals to refine what you want. Clear goals lead to vivid visualizations.

The Power of Combining Visualization with Action

Visualization is a transformative tool, but its true power emerges when paired with decisive action. Visualization sets the mental stage, aligning your thoughts, emotions, and energy toward a desired outcome, while action transforms that vision into reality. Think of visualization as the blueprint and action as the construction work that brings the blueprint to life. Use your visualizations as a guide to identify the steps you need to take, and then move forward with confidence and determination.

In the earlier example, I shared how I combined visualization with action to achieve my goals. This combination is the key because results are always a byproduct of action. Visualization alone, while powerful, is not enough. It creates focus and direction, but it is action that bridges the gap between imagination and achievement.

Here's an important realization: you're already visualizing—whether you realize it or not. Most people unknowingly visualize worst-case scenarios, reinforcing fears, doubts, and obstacles. By consciously directing your visualizations toward positive outcomes and pairing them with purposeful action, you can radically transform your life.

For me, many of the actions I needed to take came to me intuitively. Sometimes they appeared in dreams or popped into my head seemingly out of nowhere. It felt as though spiritual guidance flowed into my life the moment I became clear and determined about what I wanted to achieve. This clarity and determination are crucial because they unlock the universal principle of manifestation.

Another critical insight is to focus on "what you want," not "what you want to avoid." This distinction is essential. The universe does not discriminate between positive and negative desires—it simply manifests what you focus on most. If your energy is centered on avoiding failure or fear, you're likely to attract more of the same. Instead, shift your focus to your goals, aspirations, and dreams. Visualization, combined with clear and purposeful action, will then guide you toward the life you want to create.

Visualization also turns dreams into intentions. The important distinction is that dreams do not come true—intentions do. Dreams exist in the realm of wishful thinking, while intentions are grounded in determination and the will to act. It's natural to start with dreams, as they inspire us and expand our sense of possibility. However, until you turn dreams into intentions, those dreams will likely end in frustration. Intention is the bridge between hope and reality. So, dream big, but don't stop there. Turn those dreams into intentions by aligning your thoughts, emotions, and actions. Watch as your life improves in ways you may not have initially imagined, fueled by the clarity and commitment that only intention can provide.

Your Challenge

Today, take five minutes to visualize one of your goals. Close your eyes and create a vivid mental picture. Feel the excitement of achieving it. Then, write down one small action you can take to move closer to that vision. With consistent practice, you'll discover the immense power of your mind to shape your reality.

Now let's dive into the material in this book!

Crabs in a Bucket Mentality

As you embark on your journey of positive transformation, be mindful of whom you share your goals and aspirations with. Not everyone will be supportive, and some may even attempt to undermine your efforts—even those closest to you, such as family and friends. This phenomenon is often referred to as the "crabs in a bucket" mentality.

The "crabs in a bucket" metaphor provides a powerful illustration of a destructive dynamic that often plays out in our personal lives, social circles, and communities. If you place a single crab in a bucket, it can escape easily. However, if you add more crabs to the bucket, their collective behavior ensures that none of them get out. As soon as one crab begins to climb toward freedom, the others instinctively grab it and pull it back down, preventing its escape. This behavior, though seemingly unintentional, mirrors a pattern often found in human interactions.

In human terms, the "crabs in a bucket" mentality describes a phenomenon where individuals within a group—whether family, friends, colleagues, or a community—subconsciously or deliberately discourage others from rising above their current circumstances. This isn't always out of malice; it often stems from fear, insecurity, or the belief that someone else's success diminishes their own. However, the result is the same: progress is hindered, and the collective potential of the group is stifled.

For instance, imagine an individual in a workplace who decides to go above and beyond, taking on additional responsibilities in hopes of earning a promotion. Instead of being supported by colleagues, they are met with subtle (or overt) resistance: gossip, criticism, or even sabotage. Their efforts are undermined, not because they are unworthy, but because their ambition highlights the stagnation of others. Similarly, in social groups, a person striving to make healthier lifestyle choices may be teased or discouraged by friends who feel threatened by the implicit challenge to their own habits. Comments like, "Why are you trying so hard?" or "You're just going to fail anyway," are manifestations of the "crabs in a bucket" mentality.

This dynamic can also appear within families or cultural communities, especially when someone dares to break away from traditional roles or expectations. A young entrepreneur from a struggling background may hear discouraging remarks such as, "People like us don't succeed," or "Why can't you just be satisfied with what you have?" These comments, though perhaps disguised as concern, often stem from the fear of change and the discomfort of watching someone else strive for more.

Breaking free from the "crabs in a bucket" mentality requires awareness, resilience, and a commitment to personal growth. Recognizing the pattern is the first step. It's essential to understand that the resistance you face often has little to do with you and everything to do with others' insecurities. Your progress challenges their comfort zone, but that is no reason to hold yourself back.

Surrounding yourself with supportive and like-minded individuals can make all the difference. Seek out people who celebrate your successes and encourage your aspirations. These are the people who will lift you up rather than pull you down. At the same time, be mindful of your own actions. Avoid falling into the trap of becoming a "crab" yourself. Instead, commit to being someone who uplifts and inspires others, even if it requires stepping out of your comfort zone.

Remember, success is not a zero-sum game. One person's achievements do not diminish another's potential. In fact, when one individual rises, they often create opportunities for others to rise as well. A community of people who encourage and support each other's growth is infinitely more powerful than a bucket full of crabs pulling each other down. By choosing to break free from this mindset, you not only create a better future for yourself but also set an example that can inspire others to do the same.

Keep this in mind as you continue working through this book: be mindful of whom you choose to share your journey with, including friends and family. It's not about being secretive or deceitful; it's about protecting your progress from the "crabs" who might try to discourage you or pull you back into their bucket of excuses, inaction, and self-imposed stresses.

Positive Affirmations to Guard Against the Crabs in a Bucket Mentality of Others

Use the following positive affirmations to guard and protect yourself from those who may not have your best interest at heart.

Empowering Affirmations:

1. I am in control of my journey, and no one can pull me away from my purpose.
2. I attract supportive and uplifting people into my life who celebrate my success.
3. The opinions of others do not define me or limit my potential.
4. I release negativity and focus on the positive energy that fuels my progress.

5. I rise above criticism and remain committed to my goals.
6. My inner strength grows with every step I take toward my dreams.
7. I am unstoppable because I believe in myself and my abilities.

Resilience-Building Affirmations:

1. I am resilient and remain focused despite external distractions or resistance.
2. Challenges from others are opportunities to strengthen my resolve.
3. I choose progress over doubt, confidence over fear, and growth over stagnation.
4. I trust myself to overcome negativity and stay true to my purpose.
5. My commitment to my goals makes me unshakable in the face of adversity.
6. I am grounded in my vision and take decisive actions toward success.
7. I rise above criticism and use it as motivation to achieve greatness.

Affirmations for Inner Peace:

1. I radiate calm and confidence, unaffected by external attempts to bring me down.
2. My inner peace is unshakable, and I guard it with care and mindfulness.
3. I respond to negativity with compassion and detachment.
4. I protect my energy by focusing on what truly matters to me.
5. I remain calm and centered even in the face of external chaos.

6. My peace empowers me to make thoughtful and empowered decisions.
7. I embrace serenity and let go of tension imposed by others.

Affirmations for Strength and Positivity:

1. I am fearless, strong, and focused on achieving my dreams.
2. No one's doubts or fears can derail my journey to success.
3. I am the leader of my own life, creating a path filled with joy and purpose.
4. My energy radiates confidence and determination, inspiring those around me.
5. I release limitations imposed by others and embrace my limitless potential.
6. I am the architect of my life, and I trust in my ability to build it.
7. I rise above negativity and thrive on my journey to greatness.

Repeat each affirmation three times before moving on to the next, and maintain this practice consistently for at least 21 days. Over time, these affirmations will help establish empowering habits, enabling you to respond thoughtfully rather than react impulsively to internal or external triggers caused by the "crabs in the bucket".

What is Stress

Many people believe that stress is an external force—something that happens to us, beyond our control. This belief is not only misleading but often perpetuated by external entities, such as the media or corporations, with their own economic motives. While I won't delve into those motivations here, it's important to recognize this dynamic so you can reclaim your power. Understanding stress from this perspective can empower you to take charge of your reactions, both to internal emotions and external circumstances.

The truth is, **stress is not the problem itself—it is a symptom of a deeper issue**. Stress is a negative emotional reaction that stems from the meaning we assign to events in our lives. It's not the event itself that creates stress, but our perception and interpretation of it. In this sense, stress is an effect, not a cause. The root cause lies in the stories we tell ourselves, shaped by our imagination and beliefs. To eliminate stress, we must address these root causes, not just the symptoms. Without this inner work, the stress will persist.

When someone says, "I'm stressed," what they often mean is, "I've interpreted this situation in a way that has triggered negative emotions—fear, worry, anger, self-doubt, or even depression." These emotions cloud our ability to think clearly and distort our perspective, making it harder to make sound decisions or act effectively. Worse, they create a cycle where stress feeds on itself, compounding the emotional toll.

At its core, stress reflects the inner dialogue we carry about our experiences. It's not the event itself that creates stress, but the narrative we construct around it. For instance, a looming deadline at work isn't inherently stressful. It becomes stressful when we imagine failure, anticipate criticism, or tell ourselves we're not capable. These imagined outcomes amplify pressure and create emotional discomfort.

However, **by shifting our mindset and challenging these narratives, we gain the power to reinterpret challenges as opportunities for growth rather than threats**. This mental shift fosters resilience and cultivates an inner calm that transforms the way we navigate life's ups and downs. Stress then becomes less of an obstacle and more of a teacher—one that points us toward areas for personal growth and self-mastery.

A Personal Example: Stress and Perception

I love riding super bike motorcycles and have enjoyed it for many years. I even attended a well-known motorcycle racing school in California multiple times, honing my riding skills. While living in Japan, I found myself in a situation where I temporarily lost my driver's license. To regain my riding privileges, I had two options: take a riding test at a police-operated driving facility or attend a driving school, pass their test, and present the certificate to the police to reclaim my license.

I initially chose the police facility because it was far more cost-effective. Despite my confidence in my riding skills, I failed the test three times. Why? Because I was consumed by nerves and stress. My imagination ran wild, convincing me that the examiners were out to judge and fail me. This belief, entirely fabricated by my mind, created a self-fulfilling prophecy. I was so stressed that I couldn't perform at my best.

Eventually, I decided to enroll in the private driving school, despite the significantly higher cost. The environment was far less intimidating, and I felt calm and confident. Unsurprisingly, I passed the test on my first attempt. My riding skills hadn't changed, but my state of mind had. Calm and confidence replaced stress and fear, allowing me to succeed. This experience reinforced an important truth: stress is a creation of the mind—a reaction to how we perceive a situation, not the situation itself.

Most People Are Reaction Machines

The vast majority of us operate as reactionary beings, with our emotions and responses dictated by both internal and external stimuli. Internal stimuli, such as imagined fears or self-doubt, arise from within, while external stimuli stem from outside forces—governments, religions, media, advertisers, employers, and even friends and family. These entities, knowingly or unknowingly, trigger stress reactions in us, often motivated by a desire for economic gain or influence over our thoughts, perceptions, and decisions.

Some external influences deliberately exploit this tendency. Governments, for instance, may wield fear and anger to maintain control and division. Religions can invoke fear of judgment to ensure adherence, while news organizations thrive on sensationalism, capitalizing on fear and drama to capture attention and boost profits. Advertisers manipulate insecurities to sell products, and employers may mistakenly believe that stress drives productivity.

Even those closest to us—our friends and family—can perpetuate this cycle, albeit unintentionally. They often transmit their own reactions, shaped by the same external influences, without recognizing the impact on us. While their intentions may be good, they, too, are caught in a loop of reactivity rather than mindful action.

Breaking free from this cycle requires deliberate self-awareness and effort. By cultivating mindfulness, questioning the triggers around us, and choosing to pause before reacting, we can learn to respond thoughtfully rather than impulsively. This shift not only reduces stress but also empowers us to reclaim control over our emotions and actions. By engaging with life from a place of clarity and calm, we can break the chains of reactivity and navigate the world with intention and resilience.

Awareness: The First Step to Freedom

Awareness is the foundation for breaking free from reactive patterns and reclaiming control over your emotional responses. Recognizing that stress is not an inevitable result of external events but a reaction fueled by internal interpretations is transformative. This understanding shifts the focus from circumstances beyond your control to the inner world, where meaningful change is possible.

When you realize that stress originates in the narratives your imagination creates, you uncover the immense power you hold over your emotional state. Subconscious thoughts often dictate our perceptions and reactions, leading us to misinterpret situations as threats when they may simply be challenges or opportunities. By observing and questioning these thought patterns, you create the ability to rewrite your mental narratives, reducing stress and fostering resilience.

Awareness creates a critical space between stimulus and response—a moment of choice. This space is where transformation occurs. Instead of reacting impulsively, you can pause, reflect, and decide how to respond intentionally. Imagine a life where external pressures no longer control your peace of mind and where challenges are met with calm and clarity. That life begins with cultivating awareness of your stress triggers and reframing your responses.

Stress, after all, doesn't come from the events themselves but from the meaning we assign to them. For example, a traffic jam may irritate one person but provide another with an opportunity to relax or listen to an audiobook. The event is the same; the difference lies in perception. This demonstrates how profoundly our thoughts shape our experiences.

Developing awareness doesn't mean suppressing emotions or denying reality—it's about choosing interpretations that support your well-being. Through consistent practice, you can identify and challenge unhelpful thought patterns, replacing them with empowering beliefs. Techniques like mindfulness, journaling, and meditation are invaluable tools in this process, anchoring you in the present moment and preventing your mind from spiraling into negative scenarios.

Patience and self-compassion are essential in this journey. Improvement takes time, and every small step matters. Celebrate even minor victories, like recognizing a moment of stress and choosing to pause rather than react. Over time, these deliberate choices become second nature, rewiring your mind for calmness and clarity.

The tools and techniques shared in this book will help you neutralize stress and regain mental clarity. When you stop reacting automatically to fear, worry, and other triggers, you create space for thoughtful and intentional choices. This shift improves decision-making and enhances your overall quality of life. Challenges become opportunities for growth, and setbacks become stepping stones on the path to success.

By committing to these practices, you take control of your life. You transition from a passive participant, swayed by circumstances, to an active creator of your reality. This journey is about more than reducing stress; it's about reclaiming your freedom, peace, and joy. Though the path requires effort, the rewards—a life of balance, fulfillment, and purpose—are well worth it. Let this chapter be your starting point and take your first step forward with confidence, knowing you already possess the tools to succeed.

Moving Forward

As you embark on this transformative journey, remember this foundational truth: stress is not an external force that happens to you—it is a product of your imagination and perception. This realization is profoundly empowering because it places the responsibility and the power to improve directly in your hands.

By understanding that stress originates from within, you unlock the potential to reframe your experiences and reclaim your peace of mind. This knowledge is not about dismissing the challenges of life but about equipping yourself with the tools to face them with strength and clarity.

Through consistent practice, you'll develop the ability to pause, reflect, and respond intentionally rather than reacting impulsively. Every step you take will deepen your awareness, helping you transform stress into an opportunity for growth.

The choice to free yourself from stress is yours alone, and this journey begins with a single, courageous decision: to act. With each chapter, you'll build the skills and mindset needed to create a life of balance, purpose, and resilience.

Your journey forward is not just about eliminating stress— it's about stepping into a life of intention, clarity, and empowerment. Take that first step now, and embrace the limitless possibilities that lie ahead.

Practicing positive affirmations daily can rewire your thought patterns, fostering a calm and resilient mindset. Repeat each affirmation three times before moving on to the next, and maintain this practice consistently for at least 21 days. Over time, these affirmations will help establish empowering habits, enabling you to respond thoughtfully rather than react impulsively to internal or external triggers. Whether spoken aloud or written down, allow the affirmations' meaning to resonate deeply within you. To amplify their impact, pair this practice with meditation, anchoring the affirmations more firmly in your consciousness and reinforcing their transformative power.

Morning Affirmations to Start the Day Calm and Focused:

1. I begin this day with peace and clarity.
2. I release all worry and trust in my ability to handle whatever comes my way.
3. My mind is calm, and my heart is open.
4. I choose to focus on positive thoughts and empowering beliefs.
5. I am grounded, balanced, and in control of my reactions.
6. I face challenges with courage and composure.
7. I create my reality with thoughts of peace, gratitude, and strength.

Affirmations for Managing Stressful Moments:

1. I pause, breathe, and regain control of my thoughts.
2. I release tension and allow my mind to find clarity.
3. I respond to situations with calmness and intention.
4. Stress is a temporary feeling, and I choose to let it go.
5. I have the power to remain calm and centered in any situation.
6. My mind is my ally, guiding me toward solutions and understanding.
7. I detach from negativity and focus on what I can control.

Affirmations to Reframe Negative Thoughts:

1. I see challenges as opportunities for growth.
2. I let go of fear and embrace trust in myself and the universe.
3. I choose thoughts that serve my well-being and peace.

4. Every experience teaches me something valuable.
5. I am stronger than any trigger or stressor.
6. I release the past and focus on the present moment.
7. My inner peace is unshakable.

Evening Affirmations to End the Day with Gratitude and Calm:

1. I release the stress of the day and embrace peace.
2. I am proud of how I handled today's challenges.
3. I forgive myself for any mistakes and allow myself to grow.
4. I am grateful for the lessons today has brought me.
5. I let go of all tension as I prepare for restful sleep.
6. My mind is clear, my body is relaxed, and my spirit is at ease.
7. Tomorrow is a new opportunity to approach life with clarity and strength.

How Stress Reactions Affect Us

Stress reactions profoundly impact our health and well-being, often manifesting as headaches, high blood pressure, heart problems, depression, and other serious issues. Left unchecked, stress can escalate to tragic outcomes, including suicide.

In Japan, where I live, the prevalence of stress-related tragedies is particularly striking. Suicide by jumping in front of trains happens so frequently that it is often met with irritation rather than compassion, as daily commuters experience delays. Few pause to consider the profound despair that drives someone to such an act. Additionally, the "Suicide Forest" in Japan stands as a chilling symbol of this crisis. Many individuals travel there to end their lives, prompting regular patrols to locate and recover the deceased.

These heartbreaking patterns underscore a deeper societal issue: the lack of education and tools for managing and eliminating stress. If more people were equipped with the knowledge to address the root causes of stress, many of these tragedies could be avoided. Teaching stress management isn't just about improving individual lives—it's also a vital step toward fostering a healthier, more compassionate society.

The Fog of Stress

Stress does more than harm our physical health—it obscures our mental and emotional clarity, often more than the initial perception of the mind that caused the stress in the first place. Under stress, our perception of reality becomes distorted, making us susceptible to emotional manipulation by external influences or internal fears. Stress triggers powerful reactions like fear, worry, self-doubt, and anger, which can overwhelm rational thinking and lead to impulsive decisions.

In moments of high stress, our brains default to a fight-or-flight mode, prioritizing immediate reactions over thoughtful responses. While this mechanism was useful in prehistoric times for escaping physical threats, it often leads to overreactions in modern life. For example, during a high-stakes meeting at work, a colleague's criticism might feel like a personal attack instead of constructive feedback. Reacting defensively in the moment may strain relationships, only for clarity to reveal later that the critique was meant to help, not harm. This is how stress distorts judgment and fuels regrettable choices.

Chronic stress exacerbates this mental fog, embedding reactionary patterns into our behavior. Over time, these patterns become default responses—such as avoiding financial discussions out of fear, which only perpetuates the stress cycle. External influences, like sensationalized news or emotionally charged advertisements, further exploit our heightened emotional states, deepening the fog and making us more susceptible to manipulation.

Breaking free from the fog of stress requires awareness and intentional effort. Recognizing when stress clouds your judgment is the first step. Pausing to assess whether heightened emotions are distorting your perception can create the space needed for thoughtful responses. Mindfulness practices, like meditation or breathing exercises, help calm the mind and restore clarity. For instance, deep breathing can activate the parasympathetic nervous system, countering the fight-or-flight response, while affirmations like "I choose to respond with calm and clarity" can redirect thoughts away from reactivity.

Cultivating habits that promote mental clarity is equally essential. Journaling helps you reflect on stressful events and identify triggers. Physical exercise reduces stress's physiological effects, and practicing gratitude shifts focus away from negativity. These small, consistent practices build resilience, enabling you to navigate life's challenges with calm and confidence.

Stress does not have to control your life. By understanding its effects and using proven techniques to counteract it, you can reclaim your mental clarity and make intentional, empowered decisions. The tools in this book are designed to support you on this journey, helping you transform stress from an obstacle into an opportunity for growth and resilience.

Achieving Clarity

The first step to breaking free from the grip of stress is awareness. This awareness acts as a powerful lens through which we can examine our thoughts, emotions, and behaviors, enabling us to understand how internal and external stimuli influence our reactions. Recognizing these triggers—whether they stem from our own fears and insecurities or external pressures such as societal expectations, work demands, or relationships—is the foundation of regaining control over our minds.

When you cultivate awareness, you gain the ability to pause before reacting. This pause is where transformation begins. Instead of being swept away by an automatic stress response, you create a moment to reflect, observe, and assess the situation objectively. In this space, you can identify whether your reaction is rooted in reality or distorted by stress. For example, is the fear you feel a genuine response to an immediate threat, or is it a projection of past experiences or imagined outcomes? This clarity allows you to break free from the cycle of emotional reactivity.

Achieving clear-headedness is not an overnight process. It requires dedication, self-reflection, and the willingness to challenge habitual thought patterns. Practicing mindfulness is an effective way to strengthen this awareness. By focusing on the present moment—whether through meditation, deep breathing, or simply observing your surroundings—you can detach from the emotional intensity of stress triggers. Over time, this practice helps you see situations more clearly and respond with intention rather than impulsivity.

Clear-headedness is essential for making good decisions. When stress clouds our judgment, we often default to choices driven by fear, anger, or worry, which can lead to undesirable consequences. However, when we approach a situation with a calm and clear mind, we can analyze it objectively, weigh our options, and choose the path that aligns with our goals and values. For instance, in a heated argument, pausing to reflect can help you respond with empathy and logic rather than lashing out in frustration.

Developing this ability to observe and respond thoughtfully has profound benefits. It empowers you to navigate life's challenges with composure and confidence. You begin to trust yourself more, knowing that you can handle whatever comes your way without being overwhelmed by stress. This self-trust creates a ripple effect, enhancing your relationships, work performance, and overall well-being.

To cultivate and maintain this clarity, consistency is key. Regular practices like journaling, where you reflect on your triggers and responses, can help you identify patterns and progress over time. Affirmations and visualization exercises can reinforce a calm and focused mindset. For instance, repeating phrases like "I approach challenges with clarity and confidence" can help rewire your thoughts to align with your desired state of being.

Additionally, physical well-being plays a crucial role in supporting mental clarity. Exercise, a balanced diet, and sufficient sleep reduce the physiological effects of stress, creating a stronger foundation for clear thinking. When the body is in balance, the mind is better equipped to process and respond to stimuli in a constructive way.

In the long run, practicing awareness and achieving clarity isn't just about managing stress—it's about reclaiming control of your life. When you're no longer at the mercy of reactive emotions, you open the door to greater peace, purpose, and fulfillment. Every small step you take toward this awareness builds resilience, helping you face future challenges with strength and grace. This clarity, once cultivated, becomes a guiding light, enabling you to make decisions that lead to positive outcomes and a more empowered life.

Stress reactions are not inevitable, nor are they a permanent part of who you are. They are learned responses—patterns shaped over time by repeated exposure to specific triggers, thought habits, and external pressures. The empowering truth is that what has been learned can be unlearned. With the right tools and mindset, you can retrain your mind to approach life's challenges with calmness and clarity, replacing reactive stress with intentional responses.

This book is your guide to a transformative journey—one that dives deeper than merely managing stress symptoms. It equips you to address its root causes and take meaningful action. Through mindfulness techniques, meditation, and positive affirmations, you'll develop resilience, emotional balance, and the capacity for lasting personal growth. These practices are not just about reducing stress; they're about unlocking a profound sense of self-control and inner confidence.

Stress does not define you—it is simply a response, one that you have the power to reshape. As you move forward through this book, you'll learn to shift your perspective and recognize stress as something you can influence. This realization is liberating, placing you firmly in control of your emotional well-being. By adopting the actionable steps provided in each chapter, you'll replace reactionary habits with deliberate, value-driven actions.

Your path to purpose, confidence, and clarity begins here. With each step you take, you'll reclaim not just your peace of mind, but also your ability to thrive in the face of life's challenges.

Reclaiming Your Power

The first step in moving forward is recognizing that stress doesn't define you. While it may feel overwhelming at times, it's important to remember that you have the ability to respond differently. This process begins with awareness—mindfully observing your thoughts, emotions, and physical sensations during moments of stress. By doing so, you create the space needed to make intentional choices instead of impulsive reactions.

Next comes action. Knowledge without application is merely potential, so the tools in this book must be put into practice consistently. Even small, daily efforts can lead to significant and lasting improvements over time. For example, pausing to take three deep breaths in a stressful situation can be the first step toward reclaiming control and clarity.

Consistency is the bridge between intention and transformation. Incorporating these practices into your daily life will gradually rewire your mind to respond to stress with calmness and focus. Celebrate each small victory along the way—whether it's staying calm during a difficult conversation or letting go of a minor frustration. These moments of progress, though small, will build a foundation of resilience that allows you to face life's uncertainties with confidence and clarity.

Building a Strong Foundation

Managing and eliminating stress is not a one-time event—it's a lifelong practice. Just as a muscle grows stronger through consistent exercise, your ability to respond thoughtfully to stress will improve as you commit to these practices. Positive affirmations, for instance, help you replace self-doubt with empowering beliefs, while meditation quiets the mental noise that amplifies stress.

Journaling is another powerful tool. As you work through this book, take time to reflect on your progress, identifying patterns in your stress triggers and the positive changes you've noticed. This practice will not only help you track your growth but also reinforce your commitment to lasting improvements.

Creating a supportive environment is equally important. Surround yourself with people, habits, and spaces that encourage mindfulness and peace. Whether it's a calming workspace, a trusted friend, or time spent in nature, these external influences can complement your internal efforts, reinforcing the progress you make.

A Healthier, More Fulfilling Life Awaits

The path to managing stress isn't always easy, but it is profoundly rewarding. Imagine waking up each day feeling calm, confident, and in control of your emotions. Picture yourself navigating challenges with grace, building stronger relationships, and making decisions with clarity and focus. This vision isn't just a dream—it's a reality within your reach.

Committing to the practices in this book will help you transform your relationship with stress and develop lasting resilience. Over time, these tools will not only reduce your stress reactions but also empower you to inspire others with your calmness and clarity. The benefits of a stress-free mindset ripple outward, enriching your relationships, work, and overall sense of purpose.

The rewards extend beyond personal well-being. As you cultivate a resilient mindset, your energy will positively impact those around you. Friends, family, and colleagues will notice your calm demeanor and thoughtful responses, creating a ripple effect that fosters trust, harmony, and deeper connections in your relationships.

A Call to Action

Let this chapter serve as your call to action. The journey ahead is one of growth, self-discovery, and empowerment. Take the first step today—whether it's practicing an affirmation, setting aside time for meditation, or reflecting on a recurring stress trigger.

Remember, the present moment reflects your past choices, but the future is shaped by what you do now. Each mindful decision you make today lays the groundwork for the life you envision. Progress may not always be linear, and challenges will arise, but within each challenge lies an opportunity to grow stronger.

You have the tools and potential to transform your relationship with stress and reclaim your peace of mind. Let this be the moment you choose action over hesitation, resilience over reactivity, and clarity over confusion. The best version of your life awaits—step forward and claim it.

Positive Affirmations for Resilience Against Stress Reactions

Practicing affirmations regularly helps build emotional resilience and trains your mind to remain calm, composed, and unaffected by stress triggers. The following affirmations are written in the present tense, as if the desired state is already achieved, empowering you to internalize these beliefs and live them fully. Each line in the set of affirmations should be repeated **three times** with enthusiastic energy and a confident tone, allowing the words to resonate deeply within you. Practice this set of affirmations daily for at least 21 days to cultivate a deep-rooted habit of stress resilience.

Morning Affirmations for Starting the Day Stress-Free

1. I am calm, grounded, and unshakable, no matter what comes my way.
2. Stress has no power over me; I am in complete control of my emotions.
3. I wake up each day with clarity, confidence, and inner peace.
4. I choose to respond with calm and wisdom in every situation.
5. My mind is free of worry, and my heart is full of trust in myself.
6. I am immune to stress triggers, and I face challenges with ease.
7. I move through my day with grace, calm, and unwavering resilience.

Affirmations for Remaining Calm in Stressful Situations

1. I stay composed and clear-headed, no matter what happens around me.
2. My mind is a sanctuary of peace, untouched by external chaos.
3. I am immune to negativity and grounded in my own strength.

4. I respond thoughtfully and calmly instead of reacting impulsively.
5. Stressful situations are opportunities for me to practice calm and resilience.
6. I remain centered and confident in the face of any trigger.
7. I let go of tension instantly, allowing peace to guide my thoughts and actions.

Affirmations for Building Long-Term Resilience

1. I am resilient, and I handle life's challenges with ease and grace.
2. Stress rolls off me like water off a leaf; it cannot stick to me.
3. My calm and confidence grow stronger with each passing day.
4. I am unshakable, and nothing can disturb my inner peace.
5. My mind and body are in perfect harmony, free from stress reactions.
6. I am the master of my emotions, and I choose calmness and clarity in every moment.
7. Stress triggers are powerless against my deeply rooted resilience.

Affirmations for Internalizing Stress Resilience

1. My inner peace is unshakable, no matter what happens in the world around me.
2. I am naturally resilient, and stress cannot disrupt my clarity or focus.
3. I trust myself to handle any situation with composure and wisdom.
4. I am at peace with the present moment, and I let go of all tension.

5. My mind is clear, my heart is open, and my spirit is strong.
6. I rise above stress triggers with ease, responding thoughtfully and calmly.
7. I radiate calm, confidence, and balance in everything I do.

Evening Affirmations for Reflecting on Resilience

1. I am proud of my ability to remain calm and composed throughout the day.
2. I reflect on challenges with gratitude for the lessons they've taught me.
3. I release any lingering stress and welcome peace into my mind and body.
4. I sleep peacefully, knowing I am in control of my reactions and emotions.
5. My resilience against stress grows stronger each day.
6. I am free from worry and rest deeply in my calm, balanced nature.
7. I end this day with gratitude, clarity, and unwavering peace.

We Live in Our Imaginations

Imagination is one of the most powerful tools we possess as human beings. It bridges the gap between reality and possibility, allowing us to create, innovate, and connect in profound ways. However, this remarkable ability has a dual nature: it can uplift us, enabling creativity and growth, or it can mislead us, making us vulnerable to fear, manipulation, and self-doubt. The fact is that the subconscious mind does not differentiate between reality and imagination—what we imagine can feel just as real as what we experience. This makes imagination both a gift and a challenge.

The Role of Imagination in Our Lives

Take a moment to observe children at play. They naturally create entire worlds within their imaginations—adventures, roles, and stories that feel completely real to them. This capacity for creative visualization is part of what makes childhood so magical. As adults, we retain this power, but it often shifts toward more subtle and unconscious applications, such as planning, problem-solving, or worrying about the future.

This is where imagination can become a problem. Instead of empowering us, it can entangle us in fear, insecurity, and stress. Worse yet, many of us are unaware of how much of our daily reality is shaped not by actual events, but by the stories we create in our minds. This leaves us vulnerable to external forces that seek to exploit our imagination for their own benefit.

How Imagination is Manipulated

The power of imagination doesn't operate in isolation. It's constantly influenced by external sources—movies, music, news, advertising, and even social norms. These sources often tap into our imaginative tendencies to steer our thoughts, emotions, and actions.

Media and Entertainment

Movies, television shows, and music are among the most potent tools for engaging imagination. Through storytelling, visuals, and sound, these mediums transport us to alternate realities where we deeply connect with characters, scenarios, and emotions. While this can inspire joy and creativity, it also opens the door to subtle manipulation. Filmmakers and musicians often embed messages, consciously or unconsciously, that influence our values and beliefs. For example, a heart-wrenching movie might evoke emotions so strong that we temporarily suspend rational thought, leaving us more open to the ideas being presented.

News and Politics

The news media amplifies this effect by crafting narratives designed to provoke strong emotional reactions, particularly fear, outrage, or despair. Sensationalism is their currency because it keeps us glued to our screens. In this heightened emotional state, our ability to think critically is diminished, making us more likely to accept information without questioning its validity. Political campaigns use similar tactics, leveraging emotionally charged slogans and imagery to sway our opinions. They play on our fears, hopes, and imagined futures to guide us toward decisions that may not align with our best interests but serve their agendas.

Advertising

Advertisers are perhaps the most overt exploiters of imagination. A commercial doesn't just sell a product—it sells a vision of who we could be if we owned it. Whether it's the dream of a luxurious lifestyle, the illusion of eternal youth, or the promise of social acceptance, advertisers craft stories that make us crave what they're offering, even if we never needed it in the first place. These narratives tap into our deepest desires and fears, subtly shaping our behavior to align with corporate goals.

Religious and Cultural Narratives

Religions and cultural institutions have long understood the power of imagination. Vivid depictions of heaven, hell, divine judgment, or ultimate salvation can guide moral frameworks and actions. While these teachings can provide comfort and purpose, they can also be used to enforce compliance with institutional agendas. Fear of punishment or the promise of eternal reward can subtly—or overtly—coerce individuals into behaviors that serve institutional interests more than personal growth.

A Personal Example from Japan

In Japan, where I live, television occasionally airs emotionally charged programs designed to provoke profound sadness and tears. These programs often air in the evening, leaving viewers to carry a heavy emotional burden into their sleep. Why would a producer create content designed to manipulate emotions in this way? The answer often lies in advertising dollars—prolonged emotional engagement increases viewership, which in turn boosts revenue. This is not unique to Japan; emotional manipulation through media is a global phenomenon. However, recognizing it is the first step toward reclaiming control over our emotional and imaginative lives.

The Dual Nature of Imagination

Imagination is not inherently harmful. In fact, it is one of humanity's greatest gifts. Every invention, work of art, and scientific breakthrough began as a product of someone's imagination. Athletes visualize victory, entrepreneurs envision success, and individuals imagine better futures, turning these visions into reality. Positive imagination fuels creativity, resilience, and personal growth.

But imagination also has a shadow side. Left unchecked, it can amplify fear, self-doubt, and stress. For instance, my wife once experienced this firsthand when some of her Yoga students stopped attending her classes. She immediately imagined the worst: maybe they didn't like her teaching, or perhaps they thought her classes weren't good enough. Later, she learned the real reason—a student was simply too busy with family responsibilities. Therefore, my wife's stress had been entirely self-created in her imagination. And her behavior and beliefs reflected what she imagined until after meeting that former student who helped to break that disempowering belief that made my wife feel like she was not good enough.

Whether positive or negative, our imaginations leads us to self-fulfilling prophecies. Constantly imagining failure or rejection can lead us to act in ways that reinforce these fears. Conversely, harnessing imagination positively can lead to transformative outcomes. Visualization techniques, for instance, allow us to imagine success and align our actions with that vision, increasing the likelihood of achieving our goals. Intentionally positive visualization after all, is a form of imagination used for beneficial purposes.

Taking Control of Your Imagination

The key to harnessing the power of imagination lies in awareness and intentionality. Here's how you can take back control:

1. **Awareness:** Pay attention to your thoughts. Are you imagining worst-case scenarios, or are you focusing on positive possibilities? Simply recognizing this tendency is the first step toward positive change.

2. **Positive Visualization:** Use your imagination to picture the outcomes you desire. See yourself

succeeding, growing, and thriving. The clearer and more emotionally resonant your vision, the more powerful its impact.

3. **Mindful Media Consumption:** Be selective about the narratives you expose yourself to. Question the messages in movies, music, news, and advertisements. Are they empowering you, or are they steering your imagination toward fear or consumerism?

4. **Gratitude Practice:** Gratitude shifts your focus from what you lack to what you have. By grounding yourself in appreciation, you reduce the likelihood of getting caught in negative imaginings.

5. **Constructive Action:** If your imagination highlights a genuine concern, channel that energy into problem-solving rather than worrying. Even small steps toward addressing the issue can reduce stress and foster confidence.

Imagination as a Tool for Growth

Imagination is one of the most powerful forces you possess. It can either confine you to a cycle of stress and fear or inspire you to create a life aligned with your deepest aspirations. The choice is yours. By cultivating awareness, redirecting your thoughts, and taking purposeful action, you can transform your imagination into a tool for empowerment and growth. With practice, you'll not only reclaim control over your inner world but also unlock your potential to shape a brighter, more fulfilling reality.

Practice these affirmations consistently for at least 21 days, repeating each one three times with genuine enthusiasm and positivity. This simple yet powerful habit will create a lasting foundation that serves you positively for a lifetime.

Positive Affirmations for Harnessing Imagination

1. I use my imagination as a powerful tool for growth, success, and creativity.
2. My thoughts are aligned with positivity and constructive outcomes.
3. I consciously choose empowering narratives to shape my reality.
4. My imagination fuels my dreams and motivates me to take purposeful action.

5. I focus on the possibilities and opportunities that lie ahead.
6. I release all fears and replace them with confidence and clarity.
7. My mind is a sanctuary of hope, vision, and inspiration.

Positive Affirmations for Redirecting Negative Imagination

1. I recognize when my imagination is unhelpful and gently guide it back to positivity.
2. I see challenges as opportunities to grow and evolve.
3. My mind is free of unnecessary worries and filled with empowering thoughts.
4. I let go of imagined fears and focus on what is real and actionable.
5. I use my imagination to create solutions, not obstacles.
6. Each day, I become better at redirecting my thoughts toward joy and success.
7. I trust in my ability to reshape my reality through mindful visualization.

Positive Affirmations for Living with Intention

1. I am the author of my story and choose the narrative I live by.
2. My imagination is a source of inspiration, not stress.
3. I consciously focus on what uplifts, empowers, and excites me.
4. I take control of my thoughts and use them to build the life I want.
5. I embrace creativity and optimism as my guiding forces.

6. My imagination helps me envision and manifest a life of peace and purpose.
7. I live with awareness, choosing thoughts that align with my highest potential.

These affirmations are designed to empower and align your imagination with your desired reality. Practicing them regularly can help you reinforce constructive thought patterns and reduce unnecessary stress.

Mind Chatter: Understanding and Overcoming It

Mind chatter refers to the constant stream of unprompted thoughts that arise in our minds, often unrelated to our present activities or surroundings. This internal dialogue can be so subtle that we don't even realize it's happening, yet its effects on our emotions and overall well-being can be profound.

For instance, you might be taking a shower—a seemingly mundane and relaxing activity—when suddenly, a disagreement or argument from the past bubbles to the surface of your mind. It might be something that happened recently or even years ago, yet the vividness of the memory can make it feel as though it's unfolding all over again. If left unchecked, this random thought can spiral into a detailed mental narrative, existing entirely in your imagination, not in reality.

As this mental story develops, you may find yourself reliving the emotions tied to the original event—anger, frustration, disappointment, or even fear. To your brain and body, the emotional and physiological responses triggered by these imagined scenarios are indistinguishable from those caused by real-life events. Your heart rate might increase, your muscles tense up, and stress hormones like cortisol may flood your system, all because of a memory being replayed in your mind. Consequently, the original incident, no matter how old, gets replayed repeatedly, affecting your emotional state and even your physical well-being as if it were happening now.

The same dynamic applies to mind chatter about future events. Have you ever found yourself worrying about an upcoming presentation, an important conversation, or a looming deadline? In your mind, you may play out all the possible worst-case scenarios—forgetting your points, saying the wrong thing, or failing to meet expectations. Although none of these things have actually happened, your body reacts to these imagined fears as though they are imminent threats. Anxiety builds, and you feel the weight of stress as though the situation is unfolding in the present moment. But it is not! The danger is clear. The mind cannot distinguish between what is real and what is imagined. As a result, the emotional reaction is the same.

Why Is Mind Chatter Often Negative?

Interestingly, mind chatter tends to lean toward the negative, dramatic, and even destructive. Why is this the case? Some psychologists suggest it's a survival mechanism ingrained in us. Our ancestors needed to constantly scan for danger and anticipate worst-case scenarios to avoid threats in their environment. While this evolutionary trait was essential for survival, it's less helpful in modern life, where the "dangers" we perceive are often imagined rather than real.

That said, not all mind chatter has to be negative. There are moments when our inner dialogue is positive, constructive, and even inspiring. For instance, you might reflect on a past success or envision a bright future, which can fill you with feelings of gratitude and hope. Unfortunately, for many people, this kind of positive mind chatter is rare, while negative and fear-based thoughts dominate.

Unchecked negative mind chatter can erode your emotional resilience, sap your energy, and keep you stuck in patterns of stress and anxiety. Fortunately, there are ways to take control of your inner dialogue and redirect it toward positivity.

What You Can Do About Mind Chatter

Here are actionable strategies to address and redirect mind chatter:

1. **Practice Awareness:** The first step is recognizing when mind chatter begins. Notice when your thoughts spiral into negativity or when you replay past events or worry about the future. Mindfulness practices, such as meditation or journaling, can help you develop this awareness.

2. **Challenge Your Thoughts:** Once you're aware of your mind chatter, challenge its validity. Ask yourself:

   o Is this thought based on reality, or is it a product of my imagination?
   o Am I catastrophizing or jumping to conclusions?
   By questioning your thoughts, you create space to view them more objectively.

3. **Replace Negativity with Positivity:** When you catch yourself in a loop of negative mind chatter, consciously replace it with positive, empowering thoughts. For example, if you're worrying about an upcoming event, remind yourself of past successes and affirm your ability to handle challenges.

4. **Focus on the Present Moment:** Much of our mind chatter is rooted in the past or future. Grounding yourself in the present moment can break this cycle. Engage your senses by focusing on what you see, hear, feel, taste, or smell. This practice helps redirect your attention away from negative thoughts.

5. **Cultivate Gratitude:** Gratitude is a powerful antidote to negative mind chatter. Take a moment to reflect on the things in your life that you're thankful for, no matter how small. This simple practice can shift your perspective and help you focus on the positive.

6. **Set Boundaries for Rumination:** If you find yourself stuck in a loop of overthinking, set a time limit for how long you'll allow yourself to dwell on

a thought. After the time is up, redirect your attention to something constructive or engaging.

7. **Seek Support:** If your mind chatter feels overwhelming, consider talking to a therapist or counselor. Sometimes, an outside perspective can help you uncover the underlying causes of your thoughts and develop strategies for managing them.

Real-Life Examples of Mind Chatter

A friend once shared how he frequently found himself lost in thoughts about random events from the past. Sometimes these were actual events, like disagreements with a co-worker or a misunderstanding with his wife. Other times, they were purely imagined scenarios—arguments or conflicts that never actually occurred. Yet, the emotional reaction was the same: anger, resentment, or frustration toward the person involved, whether the event was real or fabricated by the mind.

Mind chatter can also manifest in future-oriented scenarios. A common example is rehearsing conversations or imagining worst-case outcomes before a significant meeting or event. Although these scenarios haven't occurred, the stress and anxiety they create feel real, leading to sleepless nights, irritability, or diminished self-confidence.

The Destructive Power of Mind Chatter

Unchecked mind chatter can have far-reaching consequences:

1. **Strained Relationships:** Imagined grievances can cause unnecessary conflicts and damage trust.

2. **Unnecessary Stress:** Replaying negative events creates emotional strain that can manifest physically, leading to headaches, muscle tension, or chronic conditions.

3. **Blocked Focus:** Persistent mind chatter hijacks mental bandwidth, reducing both productivity and clarity.

4. **Amplified Fears:** Negative imaginings magnify insecurities, creating a cycle of avoidance and anxiety.

Ways to Conquer Mind Chatter

Here are practical strategies to manage and quiet mind chatter:

1. **Awareness and Mindfulness:** Recognize when mind chatter arises and focus on the present moment through breathing or body scanning.

2. **Reframe Negative Thoughts:** Shift your perspective to view challenges as opportunities.

3. **Engage in Visualization:** Replace negative images with peaceful or goal-oriented visions.

4. **Practice Gratitude and Journaling:** Reflect on positive aspects of your life and write down your thoughts to identify patterns.

5. **Meditate Regularly:** Learn to observe your thoughts without attaching to them.

6. **Use Physical Activity:** Release built-up tension through movement and rhythmic exercises.

7. **Set Boundaries:** Limit overthinking by interrupting negative loops with positive affirmations.

Mind chatter is a natural part of being human, but it doesn't have to control you. By becoming aware of its presence and learning to redirect your thoughts, you can break free from its grip. These strategies empower you to restore emotional balance, enhance clarity, and achieve greater peace in your daily life. Take control of your mind chatter and transform it into a source of positivity and purpose.

Affirmations for Quieting the Mind

1. My mind is calm, clear, and focused at all times.
2. I am in complete control of my thoughts and release those that do not serve me.
3. My inner peace grows stronger with every breath I take.
4. I easily silence unnecessary chatter and focus on the present moment.
5. My mind feels light, quiet, and free from distraction.
6. I embrace the stillness within me and find clarity in it.

7. I effortlessly let go of repetitive thoughts and welcome tranquility into my life.

Affirmations for Living in the Present

1. I am fully present in this moment, free from past or future worries.
2. My attention is anchored in the here and now, where peace resides.
3. I choose to live with mindfulness and embrace the beauty of the present.
4. I trust myself to handle the future and release thoughts of what has been.
5. Each moment offers me clarity and freedom from unnecessary distractions.
6. I focus on what is real and let go of imagined fears or stress.
7. I find joy in the present and allow my mind to rest in this peaceful state.

Affirmations for Replacing Negativity with Positivity

1. I release all thoughts of worry and replace them with hope and optimism.
2. Positive, uplifting thoughts flow easily and naturally through my mind.
3. I choose to see the good in every situation and let negativity fade away.
4. My thoughts support my happiness, success, and peace of mind.
5. I allow my mind to be filled with gratitude, love, and positivity.
6. I focus on solutions and opportunities instead of imagined problems.
7. My mind is a powerful tool that I direct toward joy and fulfillment.

Affirmations for Emotional Freedom from Mind Chatter

1. I am free from the hold of repetitive and unhelpful thoughts.
2. I forgive myself and others, releasing all emotional ties to past events.
3. My mind no longer replays old stories—I am free to create a new, positive narrative.
4. I let go of thoughts that do not serve my peace or well-being.
5. I release overthinking and trust the process of life to unfold perfectly.
6. I am emotionally resilient and remain calm no matter what arises.
7. I feel light, unburdened, and at peace in my mind and heart.

Affirmations for Building Mental Clarity

1. My thoughts are organized, clear, and focused on what truly matters.
2. I find it easy to separate important thoughts from meaningless noise.
3. My mental clarity grows stronger with each passing day.
4. I have the power to pause, reflect, and choose peaceful thoughts.
5. My mind is a space of clarity, focus, and limitless creativity.
6. I make decisions with confidence and calmness, free from distraction.
7. I enjoy the quiet strength of a clear and peaceful mind.

Affirmations for Lasting Inner Peace

1. My inner peace is unshakable, no matter what happens around me.
2. I am naturally calm, centered, and in harmony with my thoughts.
3. Peace flows through my mind and body, bringing balance to my life.
4. I have a quiet, peaceful mind that supports my well-being.
5. I am free from mental noise and fully embrace the stillness within me.
6. I choose peace over worry, clarity over confusion, and calm over chaos.
7. My mind is a sanctuary of calmness, positivity, and resilience.

By repeating these affirmations daily for at least 21 days, with each line repeated 3 times, you can train your mind to release chatter and welcome stillness, clarity, and peace. For the best results, combine this practice with mindfulness techniques such as deep breathing or meditation.

Eliminate Stress by Controlling Your Mind

Controlling your mind is a skill—and like any other skill, it can be learned, refined, and mastered with effort and persistence. It requires three key elements: first, a belief or, at the very least, a willingness to experiment and discover that mastery is possible. Second, a readiness to take action. And finally, consistent practice. Through dedication and repetition, you can become an expert in managing your thoughts and emotions. When you achieve this, emotional triggers—whether internal or external—will no longer dictate your responses. Instead, you will gain the power to choose your reaction, or even to remain unshaken altogether.

The Importance of Belief and Action

Here's an example to illustrate this principle. A relative of mine once asked, "Why is it that some people succeed while others don't?" I replied, "Because some people make an effort while others make excuses." He argued, "But before someone makes an effort, they need to believe they have a chance of succeeding. They must have confidence in themselves, or they wouldn't even try." To me, that was clearly an example of an excuse. This mindset, unfortunately, led him into a cycle of inaction. He convinced himself that he lacked the confidence needed to begin and, as a result, never made an effort, fulfilling his own prophecy of failure.

I explained to him that confidence isn't a prerequisite for action—it's a result of it. You don't need an unshakable belief in your abilities before you take the first step. What you need is the willingness to act, regardless of doubts or fears. Confidence is something you build along the way as you take consistent action toward your goals. Adopting a mindset that refuses to accept failure and prioritizes perseverance transforms "trying" into "doing," which ultimately leads to success. As Yoda famously said in *Star Wars*, "Do or do not. There is no try."

From Fear to Mastery: A Personal Story

Another person I know well had a similar lesson in building confidence. She used to commute a long distance to work by bicycle but decided she wanted to switch to a scooter for convenience. After buying the scooter, she found herself terrified of riding it, overwhelmed by fears of what might go wrong. She claimed her fear stemmed from a lack of confidence, but instead of giving in, she continued to ride. Over time, her persistence paid off. With each ride, she became more skilled and less fearful, eventually gaining complete confidence. Now, she rides an 1100 cc motorcycle with ease and assurance.

The Key Lesson: Confidence Follows Action

These two stories highlight the contrasting outcomes of different approaches to fear and action. In the first, the unwillingness to act due to self-doubt led to stagnation. In the second, action in the face of fear led to confidence and success. The lesson is clear: confidence is not the starting point; it's the result of repeated effort. You don't need to believe in yourself fully to begin—you simply need to start.

Applying This to Stress Management

The ability to control your mind works similarly when it comes to managing stress. Often, stress stems from a sense of helplessness, a feeling that situations are beyond our control. But what if, instead of reacting to stress, you could pause, assess, and choose your response? Here's how:

1. **Practice Awareness:** Begin by noticing your thoughts when you feel stressed. Are they productive, or are they feeding your anxiety? Simply becoming aware of your thought patterns is the first step toward changing them.

2. **Interrupt the Cycle:** When you recognize a stress-inducing thought, interrupt it. Say to yourself, "This thought is not helpful," and shift your focus to something you can control, such as your breathing or immediate surroundings.

3. **Take Small Steps Toward Action:** Instead of being overwhelmed by the entirety of a stressful

situation, focus on one small, actionable step. For example, if a work project feels daunting, start with a single task rather than the entire workload.

4. **Build Resilience Through Repetition:** Just as the scooter rider gained confidence through practice, you can build resilience to stress by consistently choosing constructive responses. Over time, this habit rewires your brain, making calmness and clarity your default state.

The Path to Mastery

Mastering your mind isn't about achieving perfection—it's about progress. Each time you choose action over inaction, calm over chaos, and positivity over fear, you strengthen your ability to control your thoughts and emotions. Stress is not a natural part of life; it is created by how we interpret events or experiences—by how we imagine them to be. With practice, you'll find yourself better equipped to reframe challenges, respond with grace, confidence, and fearlessness, and maintain a sense of calm even in difficult situations. Even if your initial reaction results in stress, you'll learn to shut it down within seconds, moving forward with intent and resilience.

Remember, the journey begins with a single step. Start where you are, with what you have, and trust that your efforts will lead to mastery. By taking control of your mind, you take control of your life, eliminating unnecessary stress and opening the door to a calmer, more empowered existence.

Positive Affirmations for Eliminating Stress and Controlling Your Mind

Practice the following affirmations daily for at least 21 days. Repeat each line 3 times with conviction and enthusiasm. Combined with mindfulness and intentional action, these affirmations will help you retrain your mind, eliminate stress, and achieve emotional mastery:

1. I am in control of my thoughts and emotions at all times.
2. I choose peace, clarity, and balance in every situation.
3. My mind is calm, focused, and free from unnecessary chatter.
4. I respond to challenges with confidence and grace.

5. I release all stress and embrace stillness within myself.
6. I let go of fear and take consistent action toward my goals.
7. My mind works in harmony with my highest intentions.
8. I am resilient and unaffected by external triggers.
9. Confidence grows within me with every step I take.
10. I am the master of my mind, and my thoughts serve my well-being.

By practicing these affirmations consistently, you will begin to rewire your thought patterns and create a mental environment of peace, focus, and empowerment. With time and dedication, this habit will lead to profound, lasting transformation.

Many of Your Thoughts and Emotions Originate From Outside Yourself

You may have heard the saying, "Thoughts are things." While this phrase might sound metaphorical, it holds a deeper truth grounded in the nature of energy and consciousness. Thoughts are not just abstract, intangible occurrences—they are forms of energy, vibrating at specific frequencies, patterns, and rhythms. Each thought carries within it a unique "signature," much like a message encoded within a radio wave. These frequencies can travel through space, much like the signals that transmit music, images, or videos to a receiver. Just as a radio, television, or smartphone tunes into these signals to access

94

information, so too can the human mind act as a receiver for thoughts and ideas.

This phenomenon is not as far-fetched as it may initially seem. Imagine those moments when a thought or idea suddenly enters your mind, seemingly out of nowhere. Perhaps it's a memory, an insight, or even a creative spark that feels unrelated to your current train of thought. These experiences may well be examples of your mind "tuning in" to external thought frequencies. What's remarkable is that these thoughts often carry an emotional or energetic charge, which can influence your feelings, decisions, or even your perception of reality.

How Thought Transmission Works

The human brain operates as a complex bio-electromagnetic system, constantly emitting and receiving signals. Scientists have long studied brainwave activity, which consists of electrical patterns in the brain, categorized into frequencies such as alpha, beta, theta, and delta waves. Similarly, the heart, often overlooked in this context, generates its own electromagnetic field—one much stronger than the brain's. Together, these systems create an intricate web of energy that connects us not only to our own thoughts and emotions but potentially to those of others.

This interconnectedness is often unconscious. Just as a radio doesn't create the music it plays but simply picks up a broadcast signal, our minds don't always generate the thoughts we experience. Instead, they may be picking up "broadcasts" from others—thoughts, emotions, or ideas projected into the collective mental space we all share.

Real-Life Examples of Thought Reception

Have you ever been thinking about someone, only to have them call or text you moments later? Or perhaps you've experienced an uncanny alignment of ideas during a brainstorming session, where multiple people simultaneously propose the same concept? These occurrences suggest that thought transmission is not just an individual process but a shared experience.

Creative individuals often describe moments of inspiration as "downloads" or "eureka" moments, where an idea seems to arrive fully formed, without conscious effort. While it's easy to attribute this to a stroke of genius, it may also be the result of tuning into a broader field of collective thought. Writers, inventors, and artists throughout history have reported feeling as though they were simply "channels" for ideas that seemed to come from outside themselves.

Emotional Energy as a Shared Experience

Another striking example of this phenomenon occurred while I was sitting outside a busy train station in Japan. A woman with two young children—a boy and a girl—walked briskly toward a man waiting nearby. It seemed they exchanged only a few words before the man took the boy's hand. The child began crying, trying to break free, while the woman turned and hurried back to the train station without a backward glance. Watching this unfold, I suddenly felt an overwhelming wave of sadness. The emotion was so intense that it brought me to the brink of tears, even though nothing in my immediate circumstances justified such feelings.

Then it dawned on me: the woman was likely a divorced mother, and this was a custody exchange. Her hurried departure, without turning back to comfort her crying son, revealed the emotional pain she was suppressing. I realized that I wasn't experiencing my own sadness—I was picking up on hers. The moment I identified the source of this emotion as external to me, the feeling vanished as quickly as it had come.

Here is another personal example of shared emotional energy. I work 100% remotely, which means I don't need to get out of bed as early as most people to prepare for their commute. You might wonder how this relates to shared energy. Well, what do many people start their mornings with? Watching the news—a source that's often negative, dramatic, and emotionally draining.

There were mornings when I would feel sudden waves of negativity or emotional heaviness while still in bed. It puzzled me because I hadn't even begun my day. Then I made a connection: I was picking up on the emotional energy of people in my neighborhood as they started their day. Many were likely absorbing the negativity of the morning news during breakfast, unintentionally radiating those emotions into the environment. Once I recognized this, the feelings immediately dissipated.

This isn't just an example of experiencing shared emotional energy; it also demonstrates the power of awareness and detachment. By identifying the external source of the emotions and recognizing they weren't my own, I was able to let go of the feelings entirely. This highlights how mindfulness and understanding can transform your emotional experience, protecting you from the influence of external energies. It also underscores why cultivating detachment is so important.

Recognizing and Managing Thought Transmission

Awareness is the first step to reclaiming your mental sovereignty. Recognizing that not all thoughts and emotions originate from within you allows you to question their source and determine whether they serve your well-being. When a thought suddenly arises, pause and reflect: Is this truly my thought, or could it be coming from elsewhere? By cultivating mindfulness, you can develop the ability to observe your mental landscape without becoming entangled in it.

Techniques such as meditation, grounding, and affirmations can help you fine-tune your mental "receiver," enabling you to filter out unwanted frequencies and focus on thoughts that align with your values and intentions. Additionally, practicing gratitude and positive visualization can help you broadcast your own uplifting frequencies into the collective mental space, contributing to a more harmonious environment for yourself and others.

Practical Tips for Harnessing the Power of Shared Thoughts

1. **Focus Your Intentions:** When you're deeply invested in a goal or idea, take time to focus your thoughts on it with clarity and emotional resonance. Your concentrated energy may resonate with those who can help bring the idea to fruition.

2. **Maintain Positivity:** Positive thoughts carry higher frequencies and are more likely to inspire and uplift others. By cultivating optimism and confidence in your ideas, you increase the likelihood of creating a

ripple effect that aligns with your intentions.

3. **Practice Mindfulness:** Being mindful helps you discern whether a thought or emotion originates from within you or is being influenced by external factors. This awareness allows you to consciously choose which thoughts to embrace and which to release.

4. **Strengthen Your Mental Boundaries:** Visualize a protective energy shield around you. This shield should radiate the energy of love, as love is the highest vibration. When actively used, lower-level vibrations such as fear, negativity, and self-doubt cannot penetrate it. This ensures that only positive, empowering thoughts can enter, as they vibrate at a high frequency (remember, thoughts are things, energetically speaking). This practice helps safeguard your mental space from unwanted influences.

5. **Be Selective About Sharing Your Vision:** While sharing your ideas can amplify their reach and attract like-minded individuals, be discerning about whom you share with. Not everyone will be supportive, and some may attempt to discourage or undermine your efforts out of envy or negativity. Choose to share your vision with those who demonstrate genuine support, positivity, and alignment with your goals.

6. **Practice Detachment:** Once you have shared your vision or focused your intentions, release your attachment to how others react or whether your ideas are immediately accepted. Detachment allows you to maintain your peace of mind, regardless of

external opinions or outcomes. By trusting in the process and staying aligned with your inner purpose, you free yourself from unnecessary stress and remain open to unexpected opportunities and connections that align with your intentions.

Why Awareness Matters

Recognizing that not all your thoughts and emotions originate within you is crucial for maintaining your mental and emotional autonomy. Without this awareness, you may unconsciously accept external thoughts and feelings as your own, leaving you vulnerable to manipulation. Governments, corporations, the media, and even religious institutions understand this dynamic well. They exploit it to influence behavior, instill fear, and manipulate perceptions. For example, they may deliberately stress people out because individuals in a heightened state of stress are less capable of critical thinking and more susceptible to control.

However, awareness gives you the power to reclaim your mental and emotional space. When you sense that a thought or feeling isn't your own, you can consciously reject it. A simple affirmation can help:

"I recognize that this thought or emotion is not mine. I release it from every cell of my being and reclaim my peace."

With practice, this technique becomes a powerful tool for dismissing intrusive thoughts and unwelcome emotions, freeing you from their influence.

Each sentence of the following affirmations should be
repeated 3 times before going to the next sentence. Practice
for at least 21 days to enhance their potency and effect:

Affirmations for Mental Clarity and Boundaries

1. I am fully in control of my thoughts and emotions.
2. My mind is a clear and peaceful space, free from
   unwanted influences.
3. I effortlessly recognize which thoughts are my own
   and which are not.
4. I create and maintain strong mental boundaries that
   protect my peace.

5. I release all thoughts and feelings that do not align with my highest good.
6. My mind is tuned only to positive and empowering frequencies.
7. I attract thoughts and ideas that uplift, inspire, and serve my purpose.

Affirmations for Emotional Sovereignty

1. I trust my ability to identify and release emotions that do not belong to me.
2. My emotions are mine to own and manage with grace and clarity.
3. I am free from the influence of external negativity and manipulation.
4. I am deeply connected to my inner peace, no matter the external energy around me.
5. I release all emotional burdens that are not mine to carry.
6. I choose to cultivate joy, gratitude, and resilience in my emotional space.
7. My heart and mind work together to create harmony within me.

Affirmations for Intentional Thought and Energy

1. I focus my thoughts with clarity and purpose, knowing they shape my reality.
2. My mind is a powerful tool, and I direct it toward creativity and positivity.
3. I intentionally broadcast uplifting and empowering thoughts into the world.
4. I trust that the thoughts I send out align with those who can help me achieve my goals.
5. My thoughts create a ripple effect of compassion, love, and understanding.

6. I choose thoughts that bring peace and clarity to myself and those around me.
7. I am a source of positive energy that inspires and uplifts others.

Affirmations for Awareness and Releasing Influence

1. I am fully aware of the energy and thoughts I allow into my mind.
2. I instantly recognize and dismiss thoughts that are not mine.
3. I am free from manipulation and control by external forces.
4. I stand strong in my mental and emotional autonomy.
5. My awareness empowers me to make choices that align with my highest self.
6. I release stress and negativity, replacing them with peace and clarity.
7. I trust myself to navigate my mental and emotional space with confidence.

Affirmations for Positive Connection and Collaboration

1. I effortlessly align with others who share my positive intentions and goals.
2. My thoughts and ideas inspire meaningful connections with those around me.
3. I trust the flow of energy and ideas to bring me opportunities for success.
4. I am open to receiving inspiration and insights that serve my growth and purpose.
5. My mental clarity enhances collaboration and mutual understanding with others.
6. I contribute positive energy to the collective consciousness.

7. I use my thoughts to build bridges of compassion, creativity, and cooperation.

By repeating these affirmations daily for 21 days, repeating each sentence 3 times with intention and focus, you can train your mind to maintain clarity, recognize external influences, and create a peaceful, empowering mental space.

External Factors That Trigger Emotional Responses

Both positive and negative emotions are not only influenced by our own thoughts but also by external stimuli we encounter daily. These stimuli include music, movies, advertisements, speeches, sermons, news reports, and more. Often, the emotions triggered by these external factors are deliberately orchestrated by the creators of these messages to provoke specific reactions or behaviors, typically for their own benefit or agenda. This manipulation is frequently subtle, making it easy to overlook unless we cultivate conscious awareness.

However, some examples are more overt—such as fiery explosions set off during entertainment shows, like the halftime performance at a well-known sporting event. The purpose of these spectacles is often to overwhelm the senses and shut down any attempt at rational, critical thinking. Some people may argue, "Well, that's just entertaining." To that, I say, "Really? Is it?" Please take a moment to reflect and think critically about what you're consuming.

Here are a few illustrative examples:

The Santa Clause Narrative

The classic lyrics, **"He sees you when you're sleeping, he knows when you're awake, he knows if you've been bad or good, so be good for goodness' sake!"** are well-known. At first glance, it seems like an innocent holiday song. However, embedded in this cheerful tune is a clear emotional trigger: **fear**. The desired behavior? **Obedience**. The song instills a sense of accountability to an omnipresent figure, ensuring that children "behave well," not out of intrinsic motivation but to avoid judgment or punishment.

Religious Sermons

In my childhood, I often attended church services where priests would frequently emphasize the concepts of judgment day and eternal damnation in hell for those who failed to live righteously. The emotional response they sought to evoke? **Fear**. The desired behavior? **Obedience and financial contributions to the church**. By leveraging fear, these sermons effectively ensured compliance with religious doctrines while encouraging donations, often framed as a form of penance or a demonstration of devotion and goodwill.

This tactic was not isolated to one institution or denomination—it is a strategy observed throughout history in many organized religions. Fear has long been recognized as a powerful motivator, and when wielded deliberately, it can compel individuals to act against their better judgment or beyond what is truly necessary for their spiritual growth.

It's important to clarify that I am not suggesting that religion itself is inherently bad. On the contrary, religion at its core holds the potential for immense good. It provides community, moral guidance, hope, and a connection to something greater than oneself. Many people draw strength, compassion, and purpose from their faith. However, like any powerful institution, religion can also be exploited. When it is used as a tool to manipulate or control people for the benefit of a select few, that is when it becomes problematic.

The problem lies not in the faith itself but in its misuse. When fear-based tactics overshadow the core values of love, compassion, and understanding, they can alienate individuals and lead to undue psychological and emotional harm. Instead of uplifting the human spirit, such practices often weigh it down with guilt, anxiety, and a sense of unworthiness—emotions that can erode one's sense of self and autonomy.

How Fear-Based Manipulation Impacts People:

1. **Erosion of Self-Worth**: Constant reminders of judgment or eternal punishment can create feelings of inadequacy and self-doubt, leaving individuals perpetually worried that they aren't "good enough."

2. **Dependence on Authority**: When fear is the primary tool for compliance, individuals may become overly reliant on religious authorities rather than fostering their own personal connection with their faith or spirituality.

3. **Suppression of Critical Thinking**: Fear-based manipulation often discourages questioning, fostering an environment where individuals may feel hesitant to explore or critically evaluate their beliefs.

4. **Perpetuation of Guilt**: Fear of punishment often results in excessive guilt, creating an internal conflict that can negatively impact mental health and spiritual growth.

A Balanced Perspective on Faith

It's essential to differentiate between religion as a framework for personal growth and spirituality and religion as a mechanism for control. Faith, when practiced in its truest form, encourages individuals to seek inner peace, love, and compassion—not to be governed by fear. Healthy religion promotes introspection, personal accountability, and a deeper understanding of life's mysteries, helping individuals grow into the best version of themselves.

Instead of leaning on fear as a motivator, faith communities could foster understanding, love, and empowerment. A truly impactful religious teaching uplifts individuals, encouraging them to live righteously out of joy and a desire to contribute positively to the world—not because of fear of punishment.

To counterbalance fear-based teachings and reclaim your sense of spiritual autonomy, practice these affirmations daily for 21 days, repeating each sentence three times:

1. I connect with my spirituality through love, peace, and understanding.
2. My faith empowers me to grow and thrive, free from fear or guilt.
3. I embrace a higher power that inspires love, compassion, and positivity.
4. I live righteously because it aligns with my values, not out of fear of punishment.
5. My spiritual journey is guided by love and self-awareness.

6. I release all fear-based teachings and embrace the uplifting truths of my faith.
7. I am worthy of love, forgiveness, and peace, just as I am.
8. My faith fills me with confidence, clarity, and a sense of purpose.
9. I choose to focus on the positive and empowering aspects of my spiritual practice.
10. I live each day with gratitude, free from fear and full of faith.

By repeating these affirmations, you can reprogram your subconscious mind, replacing fear-based conditioning with a more balanced, empowering approach to faith and spirituality. This allows you to embrace the positive aspects of your beliefs while letting go of any undue negativity that may have been imposed upon you.

Music is one of the most profound and universal forms of human expression. It has the ability to inspire joy, evoke nostalgia, and bring about cathartic release. It can lift spirits, forge connections, and even heal emotional wounds. However, as with any powerful tool, music can also manipulate emotions in ways that are both subtle and overt.

Take my experience in a café as an example. One day, as I worked on my laptop, an inexplicable wave of sadness and depression washed over me. Just moments earlier, everything had seemed fine. The sudden shift in mood was jarring, and after some reflection, I identified the culprit: the café's playlist. It was dark and melancholic, filled with slow tempos and sorrowful lyrics. My subconscious had

111

picked up on its depressive emotional frequency, shaping my feelings without my awareness.

Once I realized this, I took action. I politely asked the staff to change the playlist. Although the next song wasn't much better, I put on my headphones and chose an upbeat, cheerful playlist of my own. Within minutes, my mood shifted back to happiness, proving the immediate and powerful impact music can have on emotional states.

This raised a disturbing question: why would a public space play such emotionally heavy music? Perhaps the staff simply enjoyed the playlist or were unaware of its emotional impact. But there's another possibility—some environments may benefit from keeping people in subdued emotional states. A somber atmosphere might encourage longer stays, contemplative behavior, or increased consumption of comfort food and drinks. Whether intentional or not, the choice of music can subtly influence customer behavior.

The Dual Nature of Music's Emotional Power

Music's ability to influence emotions is neither inherently good nor bad—it depends entirely on how it is used. On the one hand, it can lift people out of despair, enhance creativity, and foster deep social bonds. On the other hand, it can be wielded as a tool for manipulation, subtly guiding moods and decisions for someone else's benefit, often without the listener's awareness.

Marketers and advertisers understand this well. Retail stores use fast, energetic music to encourage quick purchases, while high-end boutiques favor slower, sophisticated tracks to create an exclusive atmosphere. Movies amplify tension, evoke tears, or inspire joy with carefully curated soundtracks. Even news programs pair stories with emotional music to heighten urgency, fear, or hope. These techniques aren't random—they are calculated to influence how people feel and act.

Awareness is Power

Experiences like mine underscore the importance of being aware of how music shapes our emotional states. Most of us don't question the background music in public spaces, but we should. By recognizing how it affects our mood and actions, we can regain control over our emotions.

If you find yourself feeling unexpectedly down, anxious, or overstimulated, pause and ask: Could the music around me be contributing to this? Simply identifying the source of your emotions can weaken its grip. For example, in shared spaces, you can request a change in music or put on your own headphones to counteract its effects.

Taking Control of Your Emotional State

Music's emotional power is undeniable, and while it can be manipulated to influence behavior, it can also be harnessed to support your well-being. Here's how to take control:

1. **Curate Your Playlist**: Carry headphones and create playlists that align with your goals—energetic tracks for focus, soothing melodies for relaxation, or uplifting songs for resilience. This lets you control your emotional state wherever you are.

2. **Notice Emotional Shifts**: When your mood changes suddenly, pause to observe your surroundings. Is music playing? What emotions is it evoking? Simply identifying the trigger can help

you detach from it.

3. **Advocate for Improvement**: If music in a public space negatively affects you, don't hesitate to speak up. Others might feel the same way but lack the courage to voice their discomfort.

4. **Be Critical of Media**: Recognize how music is used in movies, advertisements, and news to guide your emotions. Ask yourself whether the emotional tone aligns with the facts or if it's designed to manipulate your reaction.

The Hidden Influence of Music

Music's emotional influence isn't inherently negative, but it becomes problematic when used to exploit or control. By becoming aware of its impact, you can protect your emotional well-being and turn music into an ally rather than a hidden source of manipulation.

Remember, you are not powerless. Take control of what you listen to and how it affects you. Just as you curate the content you watch or read, you can curate the music you hear. Awareness and intentional choices will help you harness music's positive power while avoiding its pitfalls.

To strengthen your emotional resilience and maintain control over your responses to external stimuli, practice these affirmations daily for at least 21 days. Repeat each one three times with intention:

1. I am in full control of my emotions and choose how I respond to external influences.
2. Music enhances my well-being and uplifts my spirit.
3. I easily recognize and release emotions that do not align with my truth.
4. I choose to focus on positive, empowering energies that support my growth.

5. My emotional state is rooted in inner peace and strength, not external factors.
6. I am mindful of how music and media affect my emotions, and I make conscious choices.
7. I surround myself with sounds that inspire joy, clarity, and positivity.
8. I trust my ability to maintain emotional balance in any environment.
9. I create harmony within myself, regardless of external influences.
10. My emotions are my own, and I use them to create a fulfilling and joyful life.

By practicing these affirmations, you can build resilience against emotional manipulation and create an inner environment of peace and positivity, regardless of the external stimuli around you.

Control Your Emotions: Don't Let Your Emotions Control You

By now, it should be evident why mastering your emotions is essential. If it's not yet clear, consider this: unchecked emotional responses, particularly fear and anger, are powerful tools for manipulation on both personal and societal levels. They can influence everything from interpersonal relationships to international conflicts, often with devastating consequences.

Let's take war as an example. Throughout history, governments have conditioned their populations to feel fear and hatred toward another nation or group before engaging in conflict. This psychological preparation is often done over an extended period to solidify these emotions in the collective consciousness, making the public more likely to support, or even demand, aggressive action such as war or sanctions.

Consider the lead-up to the U.S. invasion of Iraq during Saddam Hussein's regime. For years, media outlets like the History Channel aired highly negative, fear-inducing documentaries about Saddam and Iraq. These programs painted a one-dimensional picture designed to provoke fear and distrust. When the tragic events of 9/11 occurred, many Americans, already primed by years of fear-based media, believed that invading Iraq was a justified response, despite Iraq's lack of involvement in the attack on the World Trade Center. Years later, it was revealed that much of the intelligence used to justify the invasion was false. Yet by then, the damage was done—countless lives lost, a country destabilized, and the seeds of long-term global conflict sown.

Had more people been equipped to control their emotions and critically evaluate the information presented to them, perhaps the public would have questioned the narrative more rigorously. Perhaps they would have rejected attempts to manipulate their fear and anger, potentially preventing the war or at least reducing its scale and impact. This is the power of emotional mastery: it not only protects you but can influence the course of history.

On a personal note, I witnessed the 9/11 attack firsthand, working just one building away from the New York Stock Exchange. My older brother worked in the second tower. Thankfully, he and his colleagues managed to escape before the collapse. In the wake of the attack, I felt an intense emotional pull to re-enlist in the Navy, driven by the belief that such a heinous act demanded a response.

However, as the dust settled and the facts emerged, it became increasingly clear that Iraq had nothing to do with the attack. So why did we send countless young men and women to kill and be killed there? What was the true agenda? And who truly benefited from that war?

It's worth reflecting on the fact that the war was not waged against Iraq as a nation but against an individual—Saddam Hussein. In the process, countless innocent Iraqi civilians lost their lives, their livelihoods, and their futures. Entire families were destroyed, and the country's economy was left in ruins. These deaths were often dismissed as "collateral damage," a cold term that attempts to sanitize the unspeakable suffering inflicted on innocent people. This is the horrifying power of emotional manipulation on a national scale, where collective fear and anger are weaponized to justify atrocities. Please, take a moment to reflect on this.

The implications of emotional manipulation extend far beyond geopolitics. On a societal level, unchecked negative emotions like fear and anger fuel hate, racism, and division. On a personal level, they can ruin relationships, lead to depression, and even drive people to suicide. These are deeply personal and compelling reasons to learn how to control your emotions.

Emotional mastery begins with controlling your thoughts. Negative thoughts, whether they originate from within or are influenced by external sources, must be acknowledged and either rejected or transmuted into something positive. This practice is not easy, but it is essential. By cultivating self-awareness and emotional discipline, you empower yourself to navigate life with clarity, strength, and compassion—unshaken by the manipulative forces that seek to exploit your emotions.

Positive Affirmations for Emotional Mastery and Resilience:

To reclaim control over your emotional responses and develop resilience against manipulation, practice these affirmations daily for at least 21 days. Repeat each one three times with full belief and intention:

1. I am the master of my emotions; they do not control me.
2. I choose to respond to situations with clarity, strength, and wisdom.
3. I easily recognize when external forces attempt to influence my emotions, and I remain grounded.
4. I transmute all negative emotions into positive energy that empowers me.

5. I release fear, anger, and doubt, replacing them with peace, love, and confidence.
6. I trust my ability to discern truth from manipulation.
7. I cultivate thoughts that uplift and align with my highest good.
8. My emotional balance strengthens my relationships and inspires those around me.
9. I remain calm and composed, no matter the external circumstances.
10. I am a beacon of positivity and resilience, untouched by fear-based narratives.

By practicing these affirmations, you can reprogram your subconscious mind, develop emotional mastery, and navigate life with a sense of empowerment and inner peace.

Improve Your Thoughts Improve Your Reality

Stress is not an inherent force in our lives; it arises from the meaning we attach to the experiences we encounter. The same situation that overwhelms one person can motivate another, depending entirely on how it is perceived and interpreted. This profound truth offers a powerful key to transforming stress into peace and clarity.

Our thoughts serve as the lens through which we view the world. If that lens is clouded by fear, doubt, or negativity, even minor challenges can feel insurmountable. Conversely, a clear, empowering mindset can transform obstacles into opportunities and setbacks into steppingstones for growth. The way we think about an experience defines its impact on us far more than the experience itself.

For example, consider a person facing an unexpected career change. One interpretation might be, *"This is the end of my stability,"* which naturally leads to stress and fear. Another perspective might be, *"This is a chance to explore new opportunities and grow,"* which inspires hope and excitement. The situation remains the same, but the thoughts surrounding it create entirely different emotional realities.

Improving your thoughts is not about ignoring challenges or pretending life is without difficulty. Instead, it's about reframing your perspective to foster resilience, courage, and clarity. By choosing thoughts that empower rather than limit, you redefine the meaning of your experiences—and in doing so, you transform your reality.

Stress is not an unavoidable burden but a reflection of how you interpret your experiences. When you master your thoughts, you gain the ability to attach new, empowering meanings to life's challenges. This shift not only alleviates stress but also paves the way for a reality filled with strength, peace, and purpose. Your thoughts hold the power—use them wisely and watch your reality transform.

The Power of Thought

Thoughts are far more than fleeting mental impressions—they are energetic vibrations that possess a profound influence over our lives. In the esoteric tradition, every thought carries a specific frequency. This frequency acts as a signal, attracting similar energies from the world around us. When we dwell on negative thoughts—whether born from hate, fear, or self-doubt—we invite a reality that reflects and amplifies these vibrations, perpetuating cycles of negativity.

On the other hand, positive, empowering thoughts emit higher frequencies. These thoughts attract energies that resonate with peace, prosperity, and joy, creating a reality that nurtures our well-being and personal growth.

This principle aligns with the timeless Hermetic axiom: *As within, so without.* It underscores a profound truth: our inner mental landscape directly shapes the external conditions of our lives. Our thoughts form the blueprint for the reality we experience, demonstrating the immense creative potential of the human mind.

Mastering the power of thought is, therefore, one of the most transformative tools we can harness. It begins with awareness—becoming conscious of the patterns of thought that dominate our minds. From there, we can intentionally choose to cultivate empowering, positive thoughts, transmuting negativity into opportunity and limitation into possibility.

By embracing this practice, we not only gain mastery over our inner world but also unlock the ability to consciously design a reality that aligns with our highest aspirations and deepest values. In essence, the power of thought is the power to create.

The Thought-Stress Connection

As already stated, stress is not a product of external circumstances; it begins within the mind, fueled by our habitual patterns of thought. Consider this: a fleeting worry about an upcoming deadline can snowball into a cascade of negative thinking—What if I fail? What will others think?—ultimately creating an overwhelming sense of pressure. This mental loop doesn't just remain in the realm of thought; it manifests physically, triggering a stress response characterized by symptoms such as a racing heart, shallow breathing, or muscle tension.

Esoteric teachings offer profound insight into this phenomenon. They remind us that stress is not an external force acting upon us; rather, it is a reaction born of perception. The way we interpret an event determines whether we experience stress or remain at peace. For example, two individuals might encounter the same challenge, but while one sees it as an insurmountable obstacle, the other views it as an exciting opportunity for growth. The difference lies not in the situation but in their respective thought patterns.

This understanding is empowering. If stress is a reaction born of perception, it means we have the ability to alter our experience of stress by changing the way we think. When we choose to shift our focus from fear to trust, from doubt to confidence, we disrupt the negative mental spiral that perpetuates stress. By adopting more balanced, constructive thought patterns, we can cultivate a sense of inner calm, even in the face of external challenges.

Transforming the thought-stress connection begins with awareness. By observing the thoughts that trigger stress, we can learn to pause, reframe, and redirect them. Practices such as mindfulness, meditation, and affirmations are invaluable tools in this process. They help us develop the mental discipline to respond to life's challenges with clarity and composure rather than with automatic reactivity.

Ultimately, by mastering the thought-stress connection, we reclaim our inner power. Stress no longer controls us; instead, we navigate it with resilience, turning potential overwhelm into an opportunity for growth and transformation. This shift allows us to live with greater peace, purpose, and presence.

Techniques for Transforming Thought Patterns

The journey to improving your thoughts and, by extension, your reality begins with awareness and intentional practice. Our minds are like gardens, where every thought we cultivate either nourishes or detracts from the overall harmony. Through the following esoteric techniques, you can learn to master your thoughts, eliminate stress, and transform your inner and outer worlds.

1. **Thought Observation:** Start with the practice of thought awareness by becoming an impartial observer of your mind. Dedicate 5–10 minutes daily to sit in silence, focusing on the thoughts that naturally arise. Don't judge or suppress them; simply observe. You might notice recurring themes, worries, or mental loops. By observing your thoughts without attachment, you create a mental buffer—a space that allows you to respond thoughtfully rather than react impulsively. Over time, this practice diminishes the intensity of negative thoughts.

2. **Positive Thought Substitution:** Your thoughts hold immense creative power, shaping both your perception and reality. When a negative or limiting thought arises, consciously pause and replace it with an uplifting or empowering alternative. For example:

- Replace "This is too hard" with "I have overcome challenges before, and I am doing so again."
- Replace "I'm not good enough" with "I am continuously growing, learning, and improving."

This deliberate rewiring of your thought patterns elevates your mental vibration, attracting more positive circumstances and outcomes into your life.

3. **Mantra Repetition:** Repeating a calming mantra can act as an anchor, centering your mind and redirecting your focus during stressful moments. A mantra such as **I am calm, capable, and aligned. No situation is an emergency unless I choose to make it so, and I choose to navigate situations with grace and ease**. works to quiet the noise of mental chatter while instilling a sense of empowerment. Commit to repeating your mantra during meditation, before sleep, or even during moments of daily stress. The rhythmic repetition gradually imprints the mantra's essence onto your subconscious, creating a reservoir of inner peace and strength.

4. **Visualization of Positive Outcomes:** Visualization is a cornerstone of mental transformation, combining the power of thought and emotion. Spend a few minutes each day vividly imagining a situation unfolding in your favor. Engage your senses—what would you see, hear, feel, or experience in your ideal outcome? For example, if you're anxious about a presentation, visualize yourself confidently delivering your message and receiving warm applause. This mental rehearsal not only soothes stress but primes your mind to attract and create the desired reality.

5. **Gratitude as a Thought Transformer:** Gratitude is one of the most potent tools for transmuting negative mental states into positive ones. Every day, write down or mentally list three things you're genuinely grateful for—big or small. Gratitude shifts your focus from lack to abundance, instantly elevating your emotional state. It's not just about the words you say but the feeling of gratitude you cultivate. When practiced consistently, gratitude reorients your mind to naturally seek out the good in every situation, making stress less dominant in your life.

6. **Mindful Breathing to Disrupt Negative Thought Loops:** Our breath and thoughts are intricately connected. When stress arises, notice your breathing—it's often shallow and rapid. To interrupt this cycle, practice slow, mindful breathing. Inhale deeply for a count of four, hold for four, and exhale slowly for six. As you breathe, imagine exhaling the tension or negativity with each breath. This simple act not only calms your body but also quiets the mind, creating space for clarity and positive thoughts. You can increase the count is you wish to do so as long as it does not cause tension. Just be mindful about keeping the proportion the same.

7. **Affirmations for Mental Realignment:** Affirmations are powerful statements that reprogram the subconscious mind. Choose affirmations that resonate with your current goals and challenges. For instance:

   - I release all stress and embrace calm and balance.
   - I am in control of my thoughts, and I create my ideal reality.

Repeat these affirmations with conviction, preferably in the morning and before bedtime, to cultivate a positive mental environment.

8. **Reframing Negative Experiences:** Shift your perspective on stressful or negative experiences by asking yourself: What lesson can I learn from this? What opportunity for growth does this present? For example, instead of viewing a mistake as a failure, see it as a valuable learning moment that brings you closer to success. Reframing transforms challenges into stepping stones, reducing stress and fostering a solution-oriented mindset.

By incorporating these techniques into your daily life, you take the first steps toward mastering your thoughts and transforming your reality. These practices not only eliminate stress but also unlock your inner potential, allowing you to navigate life with greater ease, clarity, and empowerment. As you refine your mental landscape, you'll find that the external world begins to align more harmoniously with your deepest intentions and desires.

Creating a New Reality

As you consistently implement these techniques, you'll begin to notice subtle yet transformative shifts in your life. Stressful situations will no longer feel as overwhelming, not because they've disappeared, but because you'll have redefined your relationship with them. What once triggered anxiety, or fear will now feel like an opportunity for growth or a challenge you're well-equipped to handle. This empowerment stems from your newfound ability to control your thoughts and emotions.

As your mental state shifts toward positivity and clarity, opportunities will appear to manifest more frequently. This is not a coincidence but a reflection of the energetic alignment between your elevated thoughts and the external circumstances that resonate with them. Your thoughts, whether positive or negative, create a ripple effect, shaping not only your perception of the world but also how the world responds to you. Negative thoughts lead to negative outcomes, while positive thoughts attract positive responses and results. So, why choose negativity over positivity? If you desire a positive outcome, the choice is clear: think positively. The answer is undeniable.

The more you align your thoughts with positivity, clarity, and purpose, the more your external reality will mirror these qualities. Life transforms from a reactive existence, where you feel at the mercy of circumstances, to a proactive journey of deliberate creation. Each thought becomes a brushstroke on the canvas of your life, and as you master this art, your life takes on the beauty and harmony you envision.

This is the essence of creating a new reality: it begins with your inner world. By mastering your thoughts, you gain the power to shape your experiences, relationships, and even the opportunities that come your way. Over time, you'll find that life is no longer a battleground of challenges but a dynamic, ever-evolving masterpiece that reflects your highest intentions and deepest aspirations.

Final Thoughts

The esoteric journey of transforming your thoughts and, by extension, your reality is not just a process of self-improvement—it's a profound awakening to the creative power within you. It's a reminder that you are not a passive spectator in the theater of life, reacting to external circumstances as they unfold. Instead, you are the playwright, director, and lead actor, with the ability to shape the narrative as you see fit.

By mastering your thoughts, you reclaim control over your inner world. Stress no longer defines your experiences because you recognize that its root lies in perception, not in the events themselves. This shift liberates you from the mental loops that once held you captive, opening the door to a life of clarity, peace, and intention.

But the transformation doesn't stop at stress reduction. As you align your thoughts with positivity, purpose, and gratitude, you'll find that life begins to mirror this alignment. Opportunities, relationships, and experiences that resonate with your higher state of being will naturally flow into your life. This isn't magic—it's the universal law of resonance at work. Your thoughts are frequencies, and the world responds to the vibrations you emit.

Every thought you hold is a choice, and every choice contributes to the reality you experience. This truth is both empowering and humbling. It reminds us to approach each day with mindfulness, ensuring that our thoughts are aligned with the life we wish to create.

As you continue on this journey, be gentle with yourself. Mastery doesn't happen overnight. There will be moments of doubt and setbacks, but these, too, are opportunities for growth. With patience, persistence, and practice, you'll discover that the life of peace, purpose, and fulfillment you seek has always been within your reach. It begins with a single thought—a thought that you choose wisely.

This is your life. Create it intentionally. Shape it boldly and fearlessly. And live it fully.

Positive Affirmations for Empowering Your Thoughts and Reducing Stress

Practice these affirmations daily for at least 21 days. Repeat each statement three times with intention to reprogram your subconscious mind, align your thoughts with positivity, and foster emotional resilience:

1. I am the creator of my thoughts, and I shape my reality with intention and clarity.
2. I release all stress and embrace a sense of calm and balance in my mind and body.
3. I am in control of my emotions, and I respond thoughtfully to life's challenges.
4. Every challenge I face is an opportunity for growth and self-discovery.
5. I choose empowering and positive thoughts that uplift and inspire me.
6. Stress has no power over me; I am centered, calm, and grounded.
7. I attract peace, harmony, and opportunities that align with my highest good.
8. My thoughts are a reflection of my strength, and I choose to think positively.
9. I trust in my ability to navigate life with resilience, courage, and grace.
10. I am grateful for my ability to transform my thoughts and create a fulfilling life.

By repeating these affirmations with sincerity and belief, you reinforce a mindset of empowerment, clarity, and peace, gradually cultivating habits that align with the life you desire. This practice not only rewires your thought patterns but also establishes a foundation for lasting emotional well-being and personal success.

Everyone Succeeds

There is a profound truth woven into human experience: we create or attract what we focus on the most. Whether we are aware of it or not, this principle shapes the trajectory of our lives. Every thought, emotion, and belief we hold directs the energy of our focus, setting the course of our outcomes. In this sense, everyone succeeds—even when that success may not align with traditional definitions or personal expectations.

Success is not limited to external achievements like wealth, fame, or accolades. It is the realization of the reality we nurture within. If we consistently focus on fear, self-doubt, or limitation, we unconsciously succeed in creating a life that reflects those internal states.

For instance, someone who frequently says, "I have no confidence," reinforces this belief over time, shaping their actions and leading to missed opportunities. In doing so, they inadvertently "succeed" in manifesting the reality they focus on, even though it's not the outcome they desire. In life, we attract what we focus on the most. Focus on a lack of confidence, and your life will mirror that reality. Congratulations—you've succeeded in creating a life that reflects your focus on not having confidence. Do you now see how powerful you truly are?

Conversely, when we focus on growth, gratitude, and possibility, we align ourselves with outcomes that mirror these positive energies. Imagine someone who regularly affirms, "I am capable of achieving great things." This belief shapes their actions, fostering persistence and openness to opportunities. Over time, their focus leads to achievements that reflect their confidence and determination. Congratulations—you've succeeded in creating a life that reflects your focus on confidence. Do you now see how powerful you truly are?

This principle reminds us that success is not a destination but a process shaped by the thoughts and feelings we cultivate daily. To consciously succeed, we must take responsibility for what we allow to dominate our focus. Are we nurturing thoughts that empower us, or are we fixating on fears and limitations? The answer determines the quality of our lives.

Moreover, this understanding is empowering. At any moment, we can redirect our focus toward what truly matters. We are not bound by past patterns or circumstances. By cultivating a mindset aligned with our goals and values, we can redefine success and attract the experiences we desire.

The idea that everyone succeeds reminds us of the creative power within each of us. Success is not reserved for a select few; it is inherent in all of us. The question is not whether we will succeed, but how we will define and create that success. When we focus on what drags us down or discourages us, we unlock our ability to manifest a life of fear, limitation, and depression. When we focus on what uplifts and inspires us, we unlock our ability to shape a life of meaning, fulfillment, and joy. It is your choice. So choose wisely.

Examples of Focus in Action

Because everyone succeeds, if someone consistently tells themselves, "Oh, I'm old. Oh, I'm old," their success will reflect this focus. Their repeated emphasis on age could shape their reality, reinforcing physical and mental limitations they associate with aging. They might interpret normal challenges as evidence they are "too old" to pursue goals, leading to missed opportunities and a shrinking world.

This self-talk might also affect their posture, mood, and vitality. For example, they might carry themselves in a way that reflects fatigue or resignation, further solidifying their belief. Their choices may avoid activities that could bring growth, joy, or connection, out of fear that their age makes these pursuits unattainable.

In contrast, reframing self-talk to focus on strengths like wisdom and experience could lead to a very different reality. Statements like, "I have so much to share," or "I am still learning and growing," might result in meaningful connections, new opportunities, and contributions that affirm their purpose.

Ultimately, the nature of success depends on the story we choose to tell ourselves. By focusing on limitations, success may look like creating a life bound by those constraints. Shifting focus to possibilities and strengths can create a reality filled with inspiration, vitality, and fulfillment.

The Nature of Success

To truly grasp how everyone succeeds, we must first redefine success. Society often portrays success as reaching a predefined goal—amassing wealth, achieving career milestones, or gaining recognition. While these markers are valid, they represent only a fraction of what success entails. In reality, success is the manifestation of whatever we consistently direct our energy and attention toward, whether consciously or unconsciously. As the esoteric axiom states: "Energy flows where attention goes".

This perspective reveals that success is not reserved for a select few or limited to positive outcomes. Every thought, emotion, and belief we hold contributes to the creation of our reality. When we focus on positivity, growth, and solutions, we succeed in shaping a life aligned with those qualities. Conversely, when we dwell on fear, doubt, or problems, we succeed in manifesting the very challenges we wish to avoid.

This understanding reframes success as the inevitable outcome of where we place our focus. Our thoughts and beliefs are the seeds we plant, and our external reality is the garden that grows from them. Just as a gardener chooses what to cultivate, we can nurture thoughts and intentions aligned with the life we wish to create.

Success, then, is less about external validation and more about alignment. It is the natural result of living in harmony with our values, desires, and inner truth. By aligning our focus with what matters to us, we attract experiences that reflect this alignment, creating a life rich with meaning and fulfillment.

By redefining success, we empower ourselves to take ownership of our lives. Success is not about chance or circumstance but about the choices we make—choices that determine the direction of our thoughts, the quality of our actions, and the reality we create.

The Power of Focus

Esoteric teachings remind us of a profound truth: energy flows where attention goes. This principle highlights the immense power of focus as a creative force. By consistently directing our focus toward a specific thought, goal, or emotion, we amplify its presence in our lives. Focus acts as a magnifying glass, aligning our perceptions, actions, and decisions to bring our focus into tangible reality.

Consider how this plays out in everyday life. When someone frequently envisions opportunities and remains open to them, they unconsciously align their mindset and actions to recognize and seize those opportunities. Over time, this creates a cascade of positive outcomes, reinforcing their belief in abundance and possibility.

Conversely, someone fixated on fear, doubt, or failure may unknowingly shape their reality to match those thoughts. Their focus narrows their perspective, causing them to overlook solutions, avoid risks, or make self-defeating choices. The result is a self-fulfilling prophecy that reinforces their belief in failure.

Focus itself is neutral—it amplifies whatever we direct it toward, whether negativity or positivity. To harness focus effectively, we must cultivate awareness and intentionality. Ask yourself: What am I focusing on right now? Is it aligned with the reality I wish to create? By redirecting your focus toward thoughts and goals that uplift and inspire, you take control of this creative force, shaping your life with clarity and purpose.

Focus is more than a mental habit—it is a tool for transformation. When wielded with intention, it becomes the bridge between vision and manifestation, guiding us toward a life of fulfillment and success.

Unconscious Success

One of the most intriguing aspects of focus is its neutrality—it works whether or not we are aware of it. This means our thoughts, even the unconscious ones, have the power to shape our reality. Many individuals unintentionally succeed in creating stress, limitations, or lack because their unconscious focus dwells on fear, worry, or scarcity. This automatic process highlights the power of the mind but also emphasizes the need for awareness.

At first glance, this phenomenon might seem discouraging. It suggests that we are often the architects of our own struggles, guided by unconscious patterns that no longer serve us. However, this realization is incredibly liberating. If our unconscious focus can create undesirable outcomes, it follows that intentional focus can create desirable ones. The power lies not in the focus itself but in how and where it is directed. It is akin to deciding where to shine a spotlight. Focus is therefore a spotlight. Choose to shine it on what you truly want to achieve and not on what you want to avoid. Otherwise you will invariably achieve what you want to avoid.

The path to transforming unconscious success into intentional success begins with mindfulness. By paying attention to our habitual thoughts, we can identify the underlying beliefs driving them. Are we fixated on what we lack? Do we dwell on past mistakes or future fears? Or do we focus on possibilities, growth, and gratitude? Awareness is the first step toward interrupting unhelpful thought patterns and redirecting focus toward positive, empowering states.

When we consciously choose thoughts that align with our goals and values, we harness the creative power of focus to shape a reality filled with peace, abundance, and joy. The mind becomes a tool for intentional creation rather than an unchecked source of limitation. In this way, unconscious success serves as both a cautionary tale and a reminder of the immense potential we hold.

The key is to embrace our role as creators of our experience. Every thought, whether conscious or unconscious, plants a seed in the garden of our reality. By becoming intentional gardeners—nurturing thoughts that uplift, inspire, and empower us—we ensure that our external world reflects our highest aspirations. With deliberate focus, success is not only inevitable; it becomes a reflection of the life we truly desire.

Techniques to Harness the Power of Focus

To consciously create a life aligned with your true desires, it's essential to direct your focus with intention and mindfulness. The following techniques can help you channel your thoughts effectively, ensuring your energy aligns with your goals:

1. **Clarity of Vision**: Begin by defining what success means to you. Take time to write down your goals, both immediate and long-term. Visualize yourself already living these goals, engaging all your senses. The clearer and more detailed your vision, the more effectively your focus will align with your desired outcomes.

2. **Mindful Thought Management**: Cultivate the habit of observing your thoughts throughout the day. Periodically ask yourself, *"Am I focusing on what I desire or on what I fear?"* If you notice negativity creeping in, gently redirect your attention to positive, empowering thoughts. This practice strengthens your ability to remain aligned with your intentions.

3. **Gratitude Amplification**: Shift your attention to the blessings already present in your life. Daily gratitude journaling or simply reflecting on three things you're grateful for can reorient your focus from lack to abundance. Gratitude not only elevates your mood but also creates a magnetic energy that attracts more positive experiences.

4. **Affirmations and Intentions**: Harness the power of affirmations to keep your focus aligned with your goals. Create statements that resonate with your aspirations, such as *"I am open to receiving abundance in all areas of my life"* or *"I attract opportunities that align with my highest purpose."* Repeat these affirmations daily to reprogram your

subconscious mind and reinforce a positive focus.

5. **Daily Visualization**: Dedicate a few minutes each day to vividly visualizing your ideal reality. Imagine yourself experiencing the joy, success, and fulfillment of your goals. Feel the emotions as if they are already true. Visualization bridges the gap between thought and manifestation, strengthening the connection between your focus and your future.

6. **Release Attachment to Fear**: Fear-based thoughts may arise, but they do not have to dictate your focus. When fear surfaces, acknowledge it without judgment and consciously shift your attention to solutions and possibilities. Reframe challenges as opportunities for growth and remind yourself that obstacles are temporary, but your vision is enduring.

7. **Intentional Action**: Align your daily actions with your goals. Focus is amplified when paired with deliberate, purposeful steps toward your aspirations. Whether small or significant, every action reinforces your commitment to your vision.

8. **Mindful Presence**: Practice staying present in the moment. When your focus becomes scattered or overwhelmed by future concerns, bring your attention back to the here and now. Presence enhances clarity and ensures that your energy is fully engaged in creating your desired reality.

By integrating these techniques into your daily routine, you'll cultivate the discipline and awareness needed to harness the power of focus. As you align your thoughts, emotions, and actions with your goals, you'll notice a profound shift in the quality of your life. Focus is not just a tool—it's a transformative force that empowers you to design a reality in harmony with your deepest desires.

Positive Affirmations to Increase and Improve Focus

Here are positive affirmations based on the principles of focus, stated in the present tense to help reprogram the subconscious. Use these daily for at least 21 days, repeating each one three times with intention and belief:

1. I focus my thoughts on opportunities, and they flow effortlessly into my life.
2. My attention is a powerful force, and I use it to create a positive and fulfilling reality.

3. I easily recognize the opportunities and solutions that align with my goals.
4. I am fully in control of my focus, and I choose thoughts that uplift and inspire me.
5. I attract abundance and success by directing my energy toward positive intentions.
6. My focus magnifies my success and aligns my actions with my highest aspirations.
7. I effortlessly notice and act on opportunities that bring growth and fulfillment.
8. I align my focus with clarity, purpose, and gratitude, and my reality reflects these qualities.
9. I trust the power of my focus to manifest my dreams with ease and joy.
10. Every day, my focus strengthens my connection to the life I desire and deserve.

By repeating these affirmations daily with commitment and emotion, you reinforce a mindset of clarity and purpose, aligning your thoughts and actions to create the reality you envision.

Success in Every Experience

The notion that *everyone succeeds*—even in the face of perceived failure—offers a deeply transformative perspective. If focus truly shapes reality, then every experience carries within it the potential for success, no matter how it unfolds. This idea encourages us to view life not as a series of wins and losses, but as an unbroken flow of growth, discovery, and transformation.
Failures and challenges, often viewed negatively, are merely stepping stones on the path to greater awareness and fulfillment. Every setback, heartbreak, or missed opportunity carries a hidden gift—a lesson or shift that

guides us closer to alignment with our true desires and purpose.

For instance:

- A failed relationship may serve as a mirror, reflecting areas within ourselves that need healing, while also teaching us the qualities we truly value in a partner.
- A missed opportunity might redirect us to a path more aligned with our unique strengths and aspirations, revealing the wisdom of divine timing.
- A professional setback might teach resilience and inspire creative problem-solving, ultimately strengthening our ability to thrive under pressure.

When we reframe every experience—whether joyous or painful—as a form of success, we dismantle the fear of failure. Life becomes a dynamic journey where every moment contributes to the larger tapestry of our growth, wisdom, and creation.

Embracing this Perspective:

1. **Shift from Judgment to Curiosity:** Instead of labeling experiences as "good" or "bad," approach them with curiosity. Ask, *What is this teaching me? How can I grow from this?* By doing so, you unlock the transformative power within every moment.

2. **Celebrate Progress, Not Perfection:** Success isn't a final destination—it's the continuous journey of learning, evolving, and striving toward our highest potential. Celebrate the small victories and lessons gained along the way.

3. **Trust the Process:** Life often unfolds in ways we don't initially understand. By trusting that every experience contributes to your ultimate success, you cultivate a sense of peace and resilience.

4. **Reframe Failure as Feedback:** Failure is not an end but a redirection or refinement. When we view setbacks as feedback, they lose their sting and become powerful catalysts for growth and achievement.

This mindset shifts our focus from what went wrong to what we gained, empowering us to see life as a continuous process of creation and alignment. With this perspective, every experience—regardless of its surface appearance—becomes a meaningful contribution to the masterpiece of your life.

A Collective Shift

The principle that focus creates reality does not only apply to individuals—it has profound implications for entire communities, societies, and even the world. When we extend intentional focus from personal goals to collective aspirations, we unlock the potential for massive global transformation. Just as individual focus shapes personal outcomes, shared focus has the power to shape the collective destiny of humanity.

Imagine a world where the majority of people focused their energy on values such as unity, compassion, and progress. The cumulative effect of this shared intention would generate a powerful energetic field, capable of manifesting societal harmony, innovation, and sustainable growth. This idea highlights the interconnectivity of humanity: when enough individuals align their thoughts with positive, collective ideals, the resulting synergy creates a ripple effect that elevates everyone.

The Mechanics of a Collective Shift:

1. **Shared Vision:** A collective shift begins with a unified vision of what the world could be. Whether it's eradicating poverty, promoting environmental sustainability, or fostering global peace, shared goals provide a focus point for collective energy.

2. **Amplified Intentions:** The energy of focus is magnified when more people join together with a common purpose. This is why movements for improvement—whether social, environmental, or political—gain momentum when large numbers of people align their thoughts and actions.

3. **Positive Feedback Loop:** As collective intentions begin to manifest, they inspire further participation and focus, creating a positive feedback loop. Each success fuels greater belief in what's possible, reinforcing the cycle of creation.

The Role of the Individual:

While collective shifts depend on large-scale participation, they start with individuals. Every person's focus contributes to the larger energetic field, making personal intention a critical building block for collective transformation. This means that by directing your focus toward unity, compassion, and progress, you're not only improving your life but actively contributing to a better world.

Practical Steps Toward a Collective Shift:

1. **Participate in Collaborative Initiatives:** Join groups or causes that align with your values. By combining your focus with others, you amplify the impact of your intentions.

2. **Share Positive Narratives:** Shift conversations from problems to possibilities. Share stories of progress and success to inspire others to align their focus with solutions rather than obstacles.

3. **Practice Collective Gratitude:** Gratitude isn't just a personal tool; it can be shared. Encourage communities to celebrate achievements and express gratitude for progress, fostering a collective mindset of abundance and possibility.

4. **Model Positive Focus:** Be a living example of intentional focus. Your ability to maintain a positive and solution-oriented perspective inspires those around you to do the same, creating a ripple effect.

The Greater Good: A Path Toward Collective Elevation

The concept of the greater good reminds us that our individual actions ripple outward, influencing the larger tapestry of humanity. When people collectively align their focus with shared ideals such as unity, compassion, and progress, the resulting impact is exponential. It surpasses tangible achievements and ventures into the realm of collective consciousness, shaping a world that resonates with the highest aspirations of humanity.

Elevating Collective Consciousness

Every thought, word, and action contributes to the vibrational field that defines human existence. When enough individuals focus on positive ideals, this energy coalesces, creating a momentum that uplifts societies, nations, and ultimately the world. This is not merely theoretical; history shows us how collective focus has driven social revolutions, technological advancements, and profound cultural shifts.

- **Unity through Shared Focus:** When communities work together with a unified vision, the boundaries of division—be they cultural, political, or ideological—begin to dissolve. Shared focus fosters understanding and cooperation, paving the way for collective harmony.

- **Unlocking Human Potential:** As the collective consciousness evolves, so too does our capacity to innovate, solve complex challenges, and create sustainable systems that serve all. This elevation transcends material success, touching upon the spiritual evolution of humanity.

Individual Actions as Catalysts

Every individual's focused intention becomes a building block for the greater good. By consciously aligning your actions with values that promote compassion, equity, and progress, you contribute to a shift that benefits all. Small, consistent acts of kindness or moments of intentional focus can inspire others to do the same, amplifying the impact.

Example 1: The Ripple Effect of Planting a Single Tree

Imagine a community member deciding to plant a tree in their neighborhood park. At first glance, this may seem like a minor act. However, as others notice this initiative, they are inspired to plant their own trees or contribute to beautifying the area. Over time, this collective effort transforms the park into a thriving green space, enhancing air quality, fostering biodiversity, and creating a place for social connection. What began as one person's intention grows into a shared movement, improving the environment and strengthening community bonds.

Example 2: A Workplace Culture Shift Sparked by One Person

In a fast-paced office environment, a single employee begins practicing mindfulness during lunch breaks, openly sharing how it reduces stress and boosts productivity. Curious, coworkers begin to join in, creating a daily mindfulness group. As participation grows, the practice spreads throughout the organization, influencing team dynamics. Stress levels decrease, collaboration improves, and the workplace culture shifts toward one of mutual support and mental wellness. This transformation stems from one individual's decision to align their actions with the values of self-care and shared well-being.

These examples highlight how individual actions, when rooted in intention, can catalyze broader improvements. By taking steps aligned with your values, you not only improve your own life but also inspire others to join in, creating a collective momentum toward positive transformation.

Imagine a world where the collective focus is directed toward eliminating poverty, fostering global peace, and preserving our planet for future generations. Such a vision is not just idealistic; it is achievable when individuals commit to the greater good. As this shared focus gains momentum, it creates a self-reinforcing cycle where positive outcomes inspire further positive action.

Practical Ways to Contribute:

1. **Cultivate Awareness:** Begin by understanding how your thoughts and actions influence the collective. Mindfulness in daily choices ensures that your contributions align with the values you wish to see reflected in the world.

2. **Support Collaborative Efforts:** Engage in initiatives that promote shared ideals. Whether it's volunteering, advocacy, or simply spreading positivity, your participation strengthens the collective focus.

3. **Embrace Unity in Diversity:** Celebrate differences as strengths rather than divisions. A world attuned to the greater good recognizes that diversity enriches the collective experience.

4. **Inspire Others:** Model intentional focus and action in your own life. When others witness the transformative power of your alignment, they are inspired to do the same.

A Unified Vision

The greater good is not an abstract concept but a tangible reality waiting to be realized. As individuals come together, focusing their energy on shared ideals, they create a synergistic effect that transcends what any one person could achieve alone. This collective shift toward unity, purpose, and progress is humanity's greatest potential—and it starts with the conscious choice of each individual to contribute to something larger than themselves.

By intentionally aligning your focus with the greater good, you become a co-creator of a world that reflects the highest aspirations of humanity. Together, we can manifest a future defined not by fear, division, or scarcity, but by love, unity, and abundance—a future that truly embodies the essence of the greater good.

A Call to Responsibility

When we understand that our focus acts as a magnet for our experiences, we must confront a significant realization: we are responsible for what we create. Every thought, every emotion, every belief serves as a brushstroke on the canvas of our lives. This responsibility is not a burden; it is a gift. It grants us the agency to align our focus with the outcomes we truly desire.

The Dual Nature of Success

Success, as a concept, becomes far more expansive when viewed through this lens. It is not limited to achievements or milestones. It is the manifestation of whatever we give our energy and attention to. This means that focusing on scarcity, fear, or self-doubt will bring about a form of success—but one rooted in these limiting states.

Conversely, focusing on abundance, love, and growth will yield a reality infused with these empowering qualities.

Intentional Creation

The challenge lies in choosing wisely. The human mind is a fertile ground, and whatever seeds we plant—whether positive or negative—will grow. By becoming intentional with our focus, we take control of this process. We replace unconscious patterns with deliberate creation, transforming even the smallest moments into steps toward a life of purpose and fulfillment.

A Daily Commitment

Success, in its most profound form, is not an endpoint. It is a daily practice, a series of choices made moment by moment. Each day presents an opportunity to realign our focus, to redirect our energy toward what truly matters. This practice is not about perfection; it is about persistence. It is about showing up for ourselves and our vision, even in the face of doubt or challenges.

The Question to Ask Yourself

If success is inevitable—if we are always creating something—then the most important question becomes: What kind of success will you create today? Will you succeed in cultivating joy, growth, and connection? Or will you succeed in reinforcing fear, limitation, and separation? The choice is yours, and it is a choice you make not just once, but in every thought, every action, every moment.

Each day offers countless opportunities to shape the reality you experience. The seemingly small decisions—how you respond to a challenge, the way you speak to a colleague, or the thoughts you choose to dwell on—are not insignificant. They form the foundation of the life you're building.

Example 1: Shaping Success Through Mindset

Imagine waking up and encountering an unexpected problem—a flat tire or a missed train. In that moment, you have a choice. Will you succeed in succumbing to frustration, allowing the setback to derail your day? Or will you succeed in maintaining calm, viewing the situation as a minor hiccup rather than a catastrophe? Choosing to respond with patience not only preserves your emotional well-being but also sets a tone of resilience for the rest of the day.

Example 2: Shaping Success Through Actions

Picture someone at work facing a coworker's criticism. Instead of reacting defensively or fostering conflict, they pause and consider: How can I succeed in creating understanding and collaboration? By responding with empathy and seeking common ground, they turn a potential confrontation into an opportunity to strengthen their professional relationships. This choice creates a ripple effect, fostering a more harmonious work environment.

The Power of Reflection

At the end of each day, ask yourself: What kind of success did I create today? Did my actions, words, and thoughts align with the life I want to live? By reflecting on these questions, you become more conscious of the patterns you're building and can adjust your focus toward the values and goals that truly matter.

The Ongoing Choice

The beauty of this approach lies in its simplicity and power. Success is not a distant milestone but a process unfolding in every moment. The question is not whether you will succeed but how you will define and direct that success. Will you cultivate a life of meaning, growth, and connection? Or will you unconsciously allow fear or negativity to shape your outcomes? The answer lies in the choices you make, one moment at a time.

A Journey Without End

In the end, the journey of intentional focus is not about reaching a final destination. It is about embracing the creative power within you and using it to shape a life that reflects your highest values and aspirations. It is about recognizing that success is not something to strive for—it is something you are already achieving. The question is not whether you will succeed, but how you will direct your success.

Every step you take on this journey adds to the masterpiece of your life. The path is not linear, nor is it devoid of challenges. But each moment presents a choice: to act from fear or courage, to react or respond, to focus on limitations or possibilities. It is in these choices that the true essence of your journey unfolds.

Growth as a Constant Companion

This journey does not have an endpoint because growth is infinite. As you evolve, so do your aspirations, values, and understanding of what success means. What satisfies you today may inspire you to reach higher tomorrow. By embracing this ever-changing nature, you remain open to learning, adapting, and refining your vision of what a fulfilled life looks like.

The Power of the Present

One of the profound realizations along this journey is the power of the present moment. Success is not just a future achievement—it is found in the small victories of today: the kind word you offer a stranger, the courage to step out of your comfort zone, or the clarity to focus your thoughts on gratitude instead of worry. These moments, when strung together, create a life of meaning and impact.

Infinite Possibilities

As you move forward, carry this truth with you: You are the creator of your reality. Your focus is your tool, your intention is your guide, and your life is your masterpiece. The possibilities before you are limitless because the creative force within you is boundless.

When challenges arise, see them as opportunities to strengthen your resolve. When doubts creep in, use them as reminders of your power to choose. And when you achieve milestones, celebrate them not as ends but as affirmations of your ability to shape your path.

A Legacy of Creation

This journey is not just about what you achieve for yourself but also about the legacy you leave for others. By living with intentional focus and embracing your creative power, you inspire those around you to do the same. Your life becomes a beacon of what is possible—a testament to the beauty of a journey without end.

Choose wisely, and create boldly and fearlessly. Each day is a new canvas, and you hold the brush. The journey continues, and the masterpiece is yours to create.

Final Thoughts

The notion that everyone succeeds, whether consciously or unconsciously, holds both a profound truth and a vital responsibility. It shifts the narrative from one of passivity to one of empowerment. We are not mere spectators in the theater of life, subject to the whims of external forces. Instead, we are active creators, wielding the power of our focus and intention to shape our realities.

Here are five sets of positive affirmations. Each set should be practiced for at least 21 consecutive days. For optimal impact, repeat each affirmation three times before moving on to the next. This consistent practice will help program your subconscious mind effectively and bring about meaningful improvement.

Focus and Intention

1. I focus my energy on thoughts and actions that align with my highest purpose.
2. Every day, I intentionally create the reality I desire.
3. My thoughts are powerful, and I use them to shape a positive and abundant life.

4. I direct my focus toward opportunities, solutions, and growth.
5. I am fully present, channeling my energy toward what truly matters.
6. I am the creator of my experience, and I choose my thoughts with care.
7. I trust that my focused intentions bring my dreams to life effortlessly.

Success and Empowerment

1. I succeed in creating the life I envision with every intentional thought.
2. I embrace the power within me to achieve my goals and aspirations.
3. Every step I take is a step toward success, growth, and fulfillment.
4. I align my thoughts with positivity, abundance, and gratitude.
5. I effortlessly attract the resources and opportunities I need to thrive.
6. I redefine success on my terms, and I achieve it daily.
7. I am empowered to shape my reality in alignment with my deepest desires.

Transformation and Growth

1. Every experience in my life contributes to my growth and transformation.
2. I see challenges as opportunities to evolve into my best self.
3. I am resilient, learning from every setback and rising stronger.
4. I choose to focus on solutions and possibilities, no matter the situation.

5. I transform fear into confidence and doubt into certainty.
6. I am constantly growing, evolving, and aligning with my highest potential.
7. I trust that every step I take is leading me to a brighter future.

Collective Harmony

1. My focus on unity and compassion contributes to a harmonious world.
2. I align my actions with the greater good, creating ripples of positive change.
3. I believe in humanity's potential for growth, unity, and progress.
4. Every intentional thought I have uplifts me and those around me.
5. I actively contribute to a world of abundance, love, and cooperation.
6. Together, we create a brighter and more unified future for all.
7. My focus and energy amplify the collective shift toward harmony and peace.

Conscious Creation

1. I am aware of the creative power of my focus, and I use it wisely.
2. My thoughts align with my highest aspirations, and my actions follow.
3. I create a life of peace, purpose, and fulfillment through intentional focus.
4. I trust the process of creation, knowing that my vision is becoming reality.
5. I am free from the past and fully embrace my power to create the future I desire.

6. I am aligned with the flow of abundance and opportunity in every moment.
7. I choose thoughts that uplift, inspire, and empower me to manifest my dreams.

By practicing these affirmations consistently, you will reinforce the principles of focus, intention, and creation, allowing them to integrate deeply into your subconscious and transform your reality.

Strategies For Mind Control (Your Mind)

True power lies not in controlling the external world, but in mastering the internal one. The mind is the source of all creation, perception, and transformation. Yet, without deliberate guidance, it can become entangled in distractions, dominated by fears, or trapped in patterns of limiting beliefs. This is why self-mastery—the ability to control your mind—is not just a skill but a profound gateway to realizing your highest potential.

When you control your mind, you unlock the ability to maintain clarity even in chaos, focus amidst distractions, and resilience in the face of challenges. A disciplined mind becomes your most powerful ally, enabling you to live with intention, peace, and purpose. On the other hand, when the mind remains unchecked, it tends to wander, reacting impulsively to external stimuli and creating unnecessary suffering.

In this chapter, we delve into both practical and esoteric strategies for mastering your mind. These tools are not about controlling others or manipulating external circumstances but about cultivating the inner strength to direct your own thoughts, emotions, and mental habits.

The Power of Awareness

Awareness is the cornerstone of mastering the mind. It begins with the simple yet profound act of observing your thoughts without judgment, as if you were a detached witness watching a stream flow by. This practice helps you see your mind's tendencies clearly, enabling you to recognize recurring thought patterns that might otherwise operate unnoticed.

Take a moment to pause and reflect: What patterns of thought dominate your mind throughout the day? Are they empowering and constructive, or do they subtly limit you by reinforcing fears, doubts, or negativity? Awareness gives you the power to answer these questions honestly and with clarity.

When you become aware of your thoughts, you create a vital space between your mind and your sense of self. This space is where freedom resides. It allows you to observe your thoughts objectively, rather than being swept up by them. With practice, this distance transforms impulsive reactions into thoughtful, deliberate responses, enabling you to make choices that align with your goals and values.

For example, imagine a situation where someone's comment triggers anger. Without awareness, you might react immediately and say something hurtful in return. But with awareness, you pause, recognize the emotion arising within you, and choose a response that reflects your true intentions rather than your momentary feelings. Over time, this practice strengthens your emotional intelligence and deepens your connection to your inner self.

Cultivating awareness doesn't require hours of meditation or retreating from the world. It can be as simple as checking in with yourself periodically throughout the day. Ask yourself:

- What am I thinking right now?
- How is this thought making me feel?
- Does this thought align with the person I want to become?

As you make awareness a habit, you'll notice a shift in how you experience life. Instead of being controlled by the ebb and flow of your thoughts, you'll gain the ability to steer them intentionally, leading to greater peace, clarity, and empowerment. Awareness is not just the first step to mastering the mind—it is the gateway to unlocking your full potential.

Reframing Negative Thought Patterns

Reframing is especially helpful when dealing with perceived failures, like missing a deadline. Missing a deadline does not constitute failure—it simply means you are late. Being late does not erase progress or invalidate effort. Who is to say the original deadline was even realistic? Deadlines are often set based on estimations that may not fully account for the complexities of a project or the unforeseen challenges that arise.

Consider this perspective: If the original estimate was grossly unrealistic from the start, being late is not a reflection of personal inadequacy—it's a reminder to reassess and adjust plans. The real measure of success lies not in rigidly adhering to a timeline but in your ability to persist and adapt. As long as you continue to strive toward your goal, you have not failed. Progress, no matter how delayed, is still progress.

For example:

- **Negative Thought:** "I missed the deadline; I failed."
- **Reframed Thought:** "I'm still moving toward my goal, and the deadline was just a desire that was probably not based on reality, not the final measure of success."

This perspective is empowering because it emphasizes persistence over perfection. It acknowledges that life rarely unfolds exactly as planned and that the ability to adapt and keep striving is a far greater indicator of success than adhering to an arbitrary deadline—especially one set by someone with no real understanding of whether it is achievable in the first place.

Examples of Reframing

Here are additional examples to illustrate the power of reframing:

- **Negative Thought:** "I always fail at this."
- **Reframed Thought:** "Every attempt is a valuable lesson that prepares me for success."

- **Negative Thought:** "I can't handle this."

- **Reframed Thought:** "I am stronger than I realize and capable of finding a solution."

- **Negative Thought:** "I'm behind schedule; I'll never finish."
- **Reframed Thought:** "I may be late, but I'm still making progress and learning along the way."

Cultivating a Resilient Mindset

The key to successful reframing is consistency. When a negative thought arises, pause, reframe it, and reinforce the new narrative with positive affirmations or actions that support your desired outcome. For example, if you're doubting your abilities, remind yourself of past achievements or take a small step toward your goal to build confidence.

Reframing also cultivates emotional resilience. By transforming negative thoughts into empowering ones, you train your mind to see challenges as opportunities and setbacks as stepping stones. This mindset not only helps you navigate difficulties but also enhances your overall well-being.

Progress Over Perfection

Remember, reframing is not about denying reality or ignoring genuine concerns. It's about choosing a perspective that empowers you to act, grow, and thrive. Missing a deadline or facing delays is not a failure—it's part of the journey. The key is to keep moving forward, refining your approach, and celebrating the progress you make, no matter the pace. Through practice, you'll develop a mindset that embraces possibility and positivity, enabling you to create a life aligned with your highest aspirations.

Focus and Intention

Energy flows where attention goes. This ancient principle reminds us that what we focus on expands. By directing your mind to concentrate on your goals, solutions, and positive outcomes, you harness your inner power to create the reality you desire. To ensure success, it's vital to give **NO** attention to fears, doubts, or distractions that can pull you off course. Instead, focus on what inspires and empowers you, aligning your thoughts and actions with your desired outcomes to manifest success and fulfillment.

One practical way to strengthen focus and intention is by setting daily intentions. Each morning, decide how you want to feel and what you want to achieve. For example, you might say, "Today, I will approach all tasks with confidence and patience," or "I will complete the first draft of my report with focus and clarity." Writing these intentions down in a journal or placing them on a sticky note where they remain visible throughout the day can keep you aligned with your goals.

Visualization is another powerful technique. If your goal is to excel in a presentation, spend 5–10 minutes visualizing yourself confidently delivering it and receiving positive feedback. Engage all your senses during this practice. Imagine the environment, the sound of your voice, and even the feeling of accomplishment as vividly as possible. This mental rehearsal helps reinforce confidence and clarity, making success more achievable.

Breaking tasks into smaller, more manageable goals is also highly effective. Instead of focusing on completing an entire project, direct your energy toward finishing one key section or milestone. For example, commit to completing the introduction of a report today rather than the whole document. Pair this approach with productivity methods like the Pomodoro technique, where you work in focused 25-minute intervals with short 5-minute breaks, to maintain motivation and avoid overwhelm.

Eliminating distractions is equally important. If social media or other interruptions drain your energy, consider using apps like Freedom or Focus@Will to block access during your working hours. Creating a dedicated workspace that is free from clutter and noise can also enhance your ability to focus.

Mindfulness practices can help you regain focus when distractions arise. For example, if you notice your mind wandering, take a few deep breaths and gently redirect your attention to the task at hand. Regular mindfulness practice, such as that available through my app, UMeditate, can further enhance your focus and well-being. The app offers free access to basic features for life, with optional subscriptions for advanced functionalities. However, the tools and insights shared in this book are equally effective on their own, empowering you to achieve the same transformative results without any additional resources.

Incorporating these practices into your daily routine can significantly enhance your ability to stay focused. In the morning, start your day with a simple ritual: list your top three priorities and spend a few moments reflecting on your intentions. For example, you might prioritize finishing a team report, reviewing a financial plan, and spending quality time with family. Pair this with affirmations like, "I have the clarity and energy to complete my priorities today."

When you feel your focus wavering during the day, take a moment to reset. Stand up, stretch, and take a brief walk. As you do, mentally reaffirm your intention by saying, "I am moving forward with clarity and purpose." At the end of the day, reflect on your achievements. Acknowledge what you accomplished, no matter how small, and appreciate the progress you've made. For example, you might think, "I successfully completed two tasks and made progress on the third."

By practicing these techniques consistently, you not only strengthen your focus but also align your daily actions with your higher intentions. Over time, these small but intentional efforts compound, helping you create the life you envision with clarity and purpose.

Meditation and Mindfulness

Meditation is the cornerstone of mind control. It quiets the mental chatter, strengthens concentration, and aligns your inner world with your higher aspirations. Even a few minutes of daily mindfulness practice can help you cultivate inner calm, awareness, and mental discipline.

Emotional Regulation

Your emotions are deeply connected to your thoughts. Learning to regulate emotions is an essential part of mastering your mind. Techniques like deep breathing, journaling, or simply naming the emotion you're feeling can help you process emotions constructively, preventing them from hijacking your mental state.

Visualization for Mental Mastery

Visualization is a powerful tool for training your mind. Close your eyes and vividly imagine the outcomes you desire, engaging all your senses. See, hear, and feel your success as if it's already happening. This not only primes your mind for achievement but also helps replace doubts with confidence.

Affirmations to Reprogram the Subconscious

The subconscious mind shapes much of our reality, and affirmations are a way to reprogram it. Repeat positive affirmations that align with your desired state of mind, such as *"I am in control of my thoughts,"* or *"I choose peace and clarity."* Consistency is key—repeating affirmations daily imprints them into your mental framework.

Mental Detox

Just as the body requires detoxification, so does the mind. Regularly disconnect from sources of negativity, whether it's toxic media, draining conversations, or self-critical inner dialogue. Replace them with uplifting inputs—read inspiring books, listen to empowering music, and surround yourself with supportive people.

Cultivating Discipline

Mind control requires discipline, but discipline doesn't mean rigidity. Start small by setting achievable goals for your mental habits. For example, commit to a daily gratitude practice and don't spend even a second dwelling on worries. Worries are usually the result of our imagination and have no basis in reality. If you are going to live in your imagination, as most people do, why not imagine positive experiences and outcomes instead of negative ones. Over time, these small wins build a foundation of mental strength and resilience.

Consider this example: Imagine you often find yourself consumed by thoughts of a missed opportunity. Instead of letting these thoughts spiral, you could set a simple goal to redirect your focus. Each morning, write down three things you are grateful for—big or small. For instance, you might note, "I'm grateful for a supportive friend," or "I'm thankful for a delicious breakfast."

Then, whenever worries arise, consciously choose to revisit this gratitude list. This intentional practice not only shifts your focus away from negativity but also reinforces a sense of abundance and progress in your life. Over time, these small, disciplined actions become habits that empower you to maintain control over your thoughts, even in challenging moments.

The Role of Belief Systems

Lastly, examine the beliefs that underpin your thoughts. Are they empowering or limiting? Beliefs like *"I am capable of overcoming challenges"* or *"Life supports my growth"* act as guiding principles for your mind. Challenge outdated or negative beliefs and replace them with those that align with your highest potential.

Mastering the mind is not a one-time achievement; it is a lifelong practice. But each step you take toward self-mastery brings you closer to a life of freedom, purpose, and joy. By implementing these strategies, you reclaim control over your mental landscape, transforming your mind from a restless servant to a powerful ally.

The Importance of Mind Control

The mind is among the most powerful tools at your disposal, holding the capacity to shape your reality, influence your emotions, and guide your actions. However, like an untamed wild horse, it can either lead you toward fulfillment or chaos, depending on whether it is mastered or left to roam unchecked. Without conscious guidance, the mind naturally gravitates toward fears, anxieties, and distractions. These recurring thought patterns often spiral into negative habits, hindering growth and obscuring your true potential.

Mind control is not about repressing or avoiding thoughts; it is about cultivating mastery over your mental processes. This involves developing the ability to observe your thoughts, detach from destructive mental loops, and redirect your focus toward empowering ideas and solutions. When practiced consistently, this transformation turns the mind from a restless master into a loyal servant, one that can drive you toward your highest aspirations.

Here's an important reality: if you don't take control of your mind, someone else will. Governments, advertisers, religions, employers, or even family and friends—many entities may attempt to influence your thinking. Their motives may vary, from genuine care to ideological or self-serving interests. Recognizing this helps you stay grounded, ensuring your values and integrity guide your thoughts and actions rather than external pressures.

By mastering your mind, you maintain sovereignty over your mental and emotional world, empowering you to use your resources for meaningful, positive outcomes. Instead of being swayed by others' agendas, you become the architect of your own destiny, creating a life that reflects your highest principles and goals.

Why Mind Control is Vital

1. **Liberation from External Influence:** Mastering your mind protects you from being manipulated by external forces, allowing you to think independently and align with your own truth.

2. **Greater Clarity:** A controlled mind enables you to cut through mental noise and respond to challenges with clarity and confidence, rather than impulsive reactions.

3. **Stress Reduction:** By quieting mental chatter and redirecting negative thoughts, you create space for

calm and inner peace.

4. **Enhanced Focus:** With discipline, your mind becomes a laser-like tool capable of concentrating on your goals, increasing your productivity and effectiveness.

5. **Intentional Living:** Mind mastery allows you to align your thoughts with your values and aspirations, creating a life that reflects your true purpose.

Taking Back Control

The stakes are higher than ever when it comes to controlling your own mind. In today's world, an uncontrolled mind is a prime target for external influences—from fear-based media designed to provoke panic and compliance, to manipulative advertising aimed at exploiting insecurities for profit. Even well-meaning individuals, such as family or friends, can impose their limiting beliefs upon you, shaping your perception of what's possible and acceptable in life (the crabs in a bucket mentality).

Reclaiming control over your mind is not just about personal empowerment; it's about safeguarding your ability to think freely, make authentic choices, and live a life aligned with your values. The first step in this journey is to recognize how often external influences subtly shape your thoughts, emotions, and decisions. Once you are aware of this, you can take intentional steps to disrupt these patterns and reclaim sovereignty over your mental space.

The Importance of Mental Sovereignty

The concept of mental sovereignty is rooted in the ability to take full ownership of your inner world. An untrained mind, much like an unguarded fortress, is vulnerable to outside influence. It reacts impulsively, bouncing between thoughts and emotions, often dictated by the chaos of external stimuli. This state of constant reaction leaves the mind susceptible to fear, anxiety, and doubt—fertile conditions for manipulation by external forces such as governments, religions, media, societal expectations, or even well-intentioned individuals with conflicting beliefs.

On the other hand, a disciplined mind is a source of immense personal power. It operates as a stronghold, resistant to the sway of external pressures and anchored in clarity and purpose. A disciplined mind does not allow fear or distraction to dictate its trajectory; instead, it chooses its responses deliberately and with intention. This is the essence of mental sovereignty—having the authority to decide where your focus goes, what beliefs you accept, and how you engage with the challenges of life.

The Impact of Mental Sovereignty

When you cultivate mental sovereignty, you liberate yourself from the grip of reactionary living. You move beyond being a passive participant in your life, shaped by circumstances and others' agendas, and become an active creator of your reality. Mental sovereignty grants you the clarity to:

1. **Navigate Life with Purpose:** You can make choices aligned with your goals and values rather than succumbing to societal pressures or fleeting

emotions. Every decision becomes a step toward your desired future.

2. **Resist External Manipulation:** A sovereign mind recognizes and rejects attempts to exploit your fears, insecurities, or desires. Whether it's fear-based news or manipulative advertising, you can discern these influences and maintain control over your thoughts.

3. **Foster Emotional Resilience:** With mental sovereignty, you are less likely to be thrown off course by negative emotions. Instead, you can acknowledge and process your feelings while remaining grounded and composed.

4. **Build Inner Strength:** A disciplined mind becomes a source of strength and confidence. You trust your ability to navigate challenges and face uncertainty with poise.

5. **Create a Positive Mental Environment:** By choosing empowering beliefs and nurturing constructive thoughts, you create a mental space that supports growth, creativity, and peace.

How to Cultivate Mental Sovereignty

Practicing mindfulness is a foundational step in cultivating mental sovereignty. Regular mindfulness practices, such as meditation or deep breathing, enable you to observe your thoughts without judgment, creating a mental space where you can identify patterns and choose your responses intentionally. For example, if you notice recurring thoughts of self-doubt during a meditation session, mindfulness allows you to acknowledge these thoughts and let them pass without attaching to them. Over time, this practice helps you develop clarity and emotional balance.

Questioning your beliefs is another critical aspect of mental sovereignty. Reflect on your core beliefs and examine whether they genuinely serve your highest good. Ask yourself: Are these beliefs rooted in truth, or are they inherited from societal expectations, past experiences, or external influences? For instance, if you believe, "I am not creative," challenge this assumption by reflecting on times you solved a problem creatively or tried something new. Replacing limiting beliefs with empowering ones, such as "I am capable of creative solutions," aligns your mindset with your aspirations.

Limiting negative influences is essential for maintaining a clear and focused mind. Be deliberate about the media you consume, the conversations you engage in, and the environments you inhabit. For example, if scrolling through social media leaves you feeling inadequate, set boundaries around your usage or replace it with uplifting content like inspiring books or podcasts. Surrounding yourself with supportive and empowering individuals also strengthens your mental resilience, creating a positive feedback loop that reinforces growth.

Focusing on what you can control is a powerful way to maintain mental sovereignty. Instead of fixating on external circumstances beyond your influence, direct your energy toward actions that make a difference. For example, if you're concerned about a global issue, consider how you can contribute locally or within your immediate sphere of influence. This shift from worry to action empowers you and cultivates a sense of agency.

Setting clear intentions each day acts as a compass for your thoughts and actions. Decide what you want to focus on and achieve, aligning your energy with your goals. For example, start your day by affirming, "Today, I will approach challenges with patience and creativity." These clear intentions guide your decisions and help you stay on track, even amidst distractions. Over time, this habit fosters purpose and direction in your life.

The Legacy of Mental Sovereignty

Mental sovereignty is not just about personal empowerment—it is a gift to those around you. When you master your mind, you inspire others to do the same. Your clarity, purpose, and resilience create a ripple effect, uplifting and encouraging those in your orbit to reclaim their own mental autonomy.

Ultimately, the journey to mental sovereignty is a journey to freedom. It is about reclaiming your mind as your own, free from the chains of fear, distraction, and manipulation. Instead of surrendering control of your mind to others with their own agendas and interests, you can take back control, live authentically, make deliberate choices, and create a life that reflects your highest aspirations.

Steps to Reclaim Your Mind

Cultivating self-awareness is the first step toward reclaiming your mind. Begin by observing your thoughts without judgment, taking note of recurring themes, triggers, and the impact of external influences such as news, media, music, or conversations on your mental state. This practice helps you identify patterns and gain insight into how your environment affects your mindset. Awareness is the foundation of meaningful improvements.

Limiting mental noise is another crucial step. Reduce exposure to negativity and manipulation by avoiding fear-based news, unsubscribing from advertising-heavy content, and setting boundaries with conversations that drain your energy or reinforce limiting beliefs. For example, replace your morning news with a mindful activity like journaling or reading a motivational book. Isn't that a better way to start your day than with drama and negativity?

Challenging existing beliefs is essential for mental liberation. Question the beliefs you've inherited from society, family, or past experiences, and ask yourself whether they serve your highest good. Replace limiting beliefs with empowering ones that align with your aspirations. For example, instead of holding onto the belief that "I'm not good at public speaking," adopt a growth-oriented mindset, such as "I am learning to communicate effectively and confidently."

Intentional focus is a powerful tool for reclaiming your mind. Direct your attention toward what uplifts and inspires you. Whether it's pursuing personal growth, meaningful goals, or acts of creativity, focusing on positive and constructive thoughts strengthens your mental discipline. For instance, dedicating time to a creative hobby can help redirect your energy toward activities that bring fulfillment and joy.

Practicing mindfulness and meditation is a transformative way to train your mind to remain present and resilient. These practices help you recognize unproductive thought patterns as they arise and provide tools to redirect your focus toward clarity and calm. A simple daily meditation practice, even for five minutes, can improve your ability to manage stress and maintain emotional balance.

Finally, protecting your mental energy is vital. Recognize that your mental energy is finite and precious, and invest it wisely. Prioritize activities, relationships, and content that contribute to your growth and well-being. For example, spending time with supportive friends or engaging in activities that align with your values can recharge your mental reserves and foster a positive outlook. By taking these steps, you can reclaim your mind and direct it toward a more intentional and fulfilling life.

The Ripple Effect of a Controlled Mind

When you take back control of your mind, the benefits extend far beyond personal peace and clarity. A disciplined mind empowers you to respond to life's challenges with confidence and purpose. It allows you to make decisions based on your values rather than external pressures. Moreover, your mental clarity and focus can inspire others to take control of their own minds, creating a ripple effect of empowerment and intentional living.

By reclaiming sovereignty over your thoughts, you reclaim your life. The ability to think freely, choose wisely, and act with purpose is your birthright. Taking back control is not merely an act of self-improvement—it's a declaration of independence from forces that seek to shape your reality without your consent. It is the ultimate step toward living a life of authenticity, freedom, and fulfillment.

How to Begin Cultivating Mind Control:

1. **Observe Without Judgment:** Begin by paying attention to your thoughts. Notice patterns, but

refrain from labeling them as "good" or "bad." Awareness is the first step to mastery.

2. **Replace Negativity:** When destructive or limiting thoughts arise, consciously replace them with affirmations or empowering alternatives.

3. **Limit External Noise:** Be mindful of what you consume—whether it's news, negative or emotional music, social media, or conversations. Seek inputs that uplift and inspire, rather than manipulate or distract.

4. **Set Mental Boundaries:** Establish firm boundaries for where your mental energy goes. Not every thought or opinion deserves your attention.

5. **Meditation and Mindfulness:** These practices train your mind to stay present, focused, and resilient against distractions.

When you take control of your mind, you unlock the power to design your life with intention. No longer at the mercy of others' agendas or your own unexamined fears, you become the master of your destiny. A disciplined mind not only empowers you to achieve your goals but also safeguards your freedom to think, choose, and create a life that is authentically your own.

Here are 5 sets of positive affirmations. Each set is designed to reprogram your subconscious mind and cultivate mental mastery. Repeat each affirmation three times daily for at least 21 days to establish new empowering thought patterns.

Mindful Awareness

1. I observe my thoughts with clarity and without judgment.
2. My awareness creates space for positive and intentional responses.
3. I am calm and composed in every situation I encounter.
4. I am free from mental distractions and focus on what truly matters.

5. I release all negative mental loops and redirect my energy to uplifting thoughts.
6. I trust my ability to witness and guide my thoughts effortlessly.
7. My mental clarity grows stronger with every passing day.

Empowering Beliefs

1. I am worthy of success and happiness in all areas of my life.
2. My beliefs align with my highest potential and aspirations.
3. I am free from the influence of limiting beliefs and replace them with empowering truths.
4. I am capable of achieving greatness and living my purpose.
5. I trust that my mind supports my growth and abundance.
6. I embrace change as an opportunity to expand and thrive.
7. I am in charge of creating a reality that reflects my true desires.

Focus and Intention

1. My attention is a powerful force, and I use it to manifest my goals.
2. I focus on opportunities and solutions rather than fears or obstacles.
3. Each day, I set clear intentions that guide my thoughts and actions.
4. I channel my energy into creating the life I truly desire.
5. I choose to focus on what uplifts and inspires me.

6. My focused thoughts attract positive outcomes into my life.
7. I trust the power of my intention to create meaningful improvements.

Emotional Regulation

1. I am in control of my emotions and respond to challenges with grace.
2. My emotions are valuable signals, and I process them constructively.
3. I release fear and replace it with confidence and trust in myself.
4. I choose peace over worry, and clarity over chaos.
5. Deep breathing restores my calm and focus whenever I need it.
6. I am resilient and handle stress with strength and ease.
7. My emotional balance empowers me to create a fulfilling life.

Mental Sovereignty

1. I am the master of my mind and direct my thoughts with purpose.
2. My mind is a fortress, immune to external manipulation.
3. I think freely and make authentic choices that align with my truth.
4. My thoughts are my own, and I guard them with awareness and care.
5. I release the need for approval and trust my inner wisdom.
6. I create mental boundaries that protect my focus and energy.

7. My mental sovereignty empowers me to live a life of freedom and fulfillment.

By repeating these affirmations consistently, you will align your thoughts, emotions, and intentions with your highest aspirations, gaining control over your mind and the life you wish to create.

Overcoming Common Challenges

Even with dedication and practice, the path to mastering your mind is not without its hurdles. These challenges are natural and offer valuable opportunities for growth. By addressing them with intentional strategies, you can stay on course and deepen your mental discipline.

Dealing with overthinking can feel like an endless loop of draining thoughts. To overcome this, practice grounding techniques. Focus on your breath by taking slow, deep breaths—inhaling for a count of four, holding for four, and exhaling for six (do this 7 times in a row). This will calm you.

Alternatively, engage your senses by noticing three things you can see, hear, and feel. These techniques shift your focus from your thoughts to the present moment, breaking the cycle of mental overactivity and restoring clarity.

Breaking negative loops often requires physical action to reset your mind. Negative thought patterns can spiral into self-doubt, fear, or frustration, but physically changing your state can help. Stand up and stretch, focusing on areas of tension, or take a brisk walk outdoors to refresh your perspective. Shaking out your hands or moving your body releases stagnant energy, disrupting mental patterns and allowing you to redirect focus toward positive outcomes.

Standing tall with your back straight, shoulders back, and chest out can also induce a sense of confidence, eliminating self-doubt. Experiment with these techniques and discover what works best for you.

Staying consistent is foundational to developing any habit, including mastering your mind. Begin with small, achievable goals, such as dedicating just five minutes daily to mindfulness activities like meditation, journaling, or affirmations. Use reminders like alarms or sticky notes to stay on track, and journal your progress to celebrate small wins. Incremental progress builds confidence and momentum, making it easier to sustain your commitment.

Navigating emotional triggers is critical for maintaining focus. Strong emotions can hijack your mental state, leading to impulsive reactions. When triggered, pause and name the emotion you're experiencing—whether it's anger, sadness, or frustration. Practice calming techniques, such as deep breathing or repeating affirmations like "I choose peace." Reflect on the situation afterward to identify its root cause and explore ways to respond differently in the future. This approach helps you regain control and strengthen emotional resilience.

Overcoming self-doubt requires shifting your internal dialogue. Self-doubt can creep in, questioning your ability to master your mind or achieve your goals. Counteract this with affirmations like "I am capable of growth and transformation" or "Every step I take brings me closer to mastery." Reflecting on past successes also reinforces your resilience and replaces doubt with trust in your journey.

Managing external distractions is essential in today's fast-paced world. Constant notifications and noisy environments can easily derail your focus. Create a distraction-free zone by silencing your phone or using focus apps during mental discipline time. Choose a quiet, comfortable space where you can concentrate uninterrupted. A controlled environment supports deeper focus, enabling you to achieve greater clarity and productivity.

Reframing setbacks as learning opportunities is key to staying motivated. It's easy to feel discouraged when progress seems slow. Instead, view setbacks as valuable lessons. Ask yourself, "What can I learn from this experience?" Celebrate the fact that you noticed the setback—awareness is itself progress. This mindset turns challenges into stepping stones, keeping you motivated and resilient.

Finally, dealing with impatience is essential for long-term success. Frustration may arise when results aren't immediate. Practice patience by focusing on the progress you've made rather than what remains. Incorporate mindfulness practices to emphasize being present in the moment. Patience ensures gradual, sustainable growth, allowing transformation to unfold naturally.

Mastering your mind is a process, not a destination. Challenges are inevitable, but they offer opportunities to strengthen your mental discipline and resilience. By approaching these obstacles with practical strategies and a growth mindset, you'll make steady progress toward clarity, focus, and self-mastery. Each step forward is a testament to your commitment to personal transformation.

The Rewards of Mind Control

Mastering your mind is one of the most empowering achievements you can strive for. It grants you the ability to shape your thoughts, actions, and emotions in alignment with your highest aspirations. By taking control of your inner world, you unlock the potential to live a life filled with purpose, clarity, and resilience. Below are the profound rewards that come with cultivating mind control.

A controlled mind equips you to navigate challenges with resilience and calm. Life is unpredictable, and obstacles are inevitable, but by mastering your mind, you face these hurdles with unwavering composure. Instead of reacting impulsively, you respond thoughtfully, seeing opportunities for growth and solutions rather than problems. This resilience not only helps you overcome difficulties but also strengthens your confidence in your ability to handle future challenges.

In today's world full of distractions, the ability to stay focused on your goals is a superpower. Mind control enables you to direct your energy toward what truly matters. You remain steadfast in your pursuit of goals, prioritizing meaningful tasks over fleeting distractions. This focus accelerates your progress, ensuring that your efforts align with your long-term vision, making every step deliberate and impactful.

Stress often results from unmanaged thoughts, but by mastering your mind, you learn to transform stress into clarity and creativity. Rather than allowing stress to overwhelm you, it becomes a catalyst for innovation and productivity. You approach problems with a creative mindset, finding solutions where others see roadblocks. This ability transforms challenges into opportunities, enhancing both your personal and professional life.

Your mind is the architect of your reality, and when you control your thoughts, you cultivate a life aligned with your highest intentions. By focusing on positive and empowering intentions, you attract experiences, relationships, and opportunities that resonate with your values and desires. This alignment fosters a sense of fulfillment and harmony, allowing you to live authentically and joyfully.

A disciplined mind enhances your emotional intelligence, helping you understand and regulate your emotions more effectively. With this skill, you respond to emotional triggers with wisdom and empathy, fostering healthier and more meaningful relationships. Emotional intelligence also strengthens decision-making, enriching both personal and professional interactions and ensuring that your connections are built on mutual understanding.

Mind control quiets the mental chatter that often fuels anxiety and dissatisfaction, allowing you to strengthen your inner peace and contentment. By silencing the noise of unnecessary worries, you develop an unshakable peace that isn't dependent on external circumstances. This contentment becomes a constant source of strength and joy, enabling you to navigate life's ups and downs with grace while maintaining balance and well-being.

When you master your mind, you naturally inspire others to do the same. Your clarity, focus, and calm demeanor serve as a powerful example, encouraging those around you to cultivate their own mental discipline. This ripple effect creates a supportive and empowered community, amplifying the collective potential for growth and transformation, proving that individual mastery benefits everyone.

By embracing these rewards, you open the door to a life of intentionality, resilience, and fulfillment. Mastering your mind not only transforms your personal journey but also uplifts those around you, creating a ripple effect of empowerment and growth.

Progress Over Perfection

Mind control is not about achieving perfection—it's about making consistent progress. Each small step, whether it's observing your thoughts, practicing mindfulness, or setting daily intentions, builds your capacity for self-mastery.

Why It Matters: Every effort you make contributes to a stronger foundation, allowing you to navigate life with greater ease and purpose. Remember, growth is a journey, and every step forward is a victory worth celebrating.

When you control your mind, you don't just control your life—you transform it. The rewards of mind control extend beyond personal success; they enrich your relationships, elevate your impact, and align your existence with your highest potential. By committing to this practice, you unlock a life of intention, fulfillment, and boundless possibilities.

Each time you practice these affirmations, **repeat each line 3 times** with focus and intention. Practice this daily for at least **21 days** to replace old programming with empowering new beliefs.

Awareness and Observation

1. I am fully aware of my thoughts and observe them without judgment.
2. My awareness illuminates my mental patterns, guiding me toward clarity.
3. I recognize and release thought habits that no longer serve me.
4. I am the observer of my mind, not a victim of its chatter.

191

5. Each day, I grow more present and mindful of the now.
6. I notice triggers calmly and respond thoughtfully with wisdom.
7. My awareness empowers me to choose empowering thoughts.

Discipline and Focus

1. I train my mind with discipline, strengthening it daily.
2. Distractions hold no power over me—I focus on what matters most.
3. Consistency fuels my mental strength and growth.
4. My mind is a powerful tool, and I direct it with purpose.
5. I practice discipline with grace, allowing progress over perfection.
6. Each focused thought brings me closer to my goals.
7. I am in full control of my mental energy, guarding it wisely.

Intentional Living

1. I set clear intentions that align with my highest values.
2. My thoughts and actions reflect the life I wish to create.
3. Each day begins with purpose, guided by my inner vision.
4. I live intentionally, creating a meaningful and fulfilled life.
5. My goals are clear, and I direct my energy toward achieving them.
6. I align my thoughts with gratitude, peace, and determination.

7. I design my reality with intention, clarity, and focus.

Emotional Mastery and Resilience

1. I respond to challenges with resilience and calm.
2. My emotions flow freely, but I choose how to navigate them.
3. Stress transforms into clarity and creativity within me.
4. I breathe deeply and return to peace in moments of intensity.
5. I welcome each emotion as a guide, not a dictator.
6. I cultivate inner calm, regardless of external circumstances.
7. My emotional intelligence strengthens my connections and decisions.

Gratitude and Positive Affirmations

1. I am grateful for the abundance in my life and the growth within me.
2. My thoughts are positive, uplifting, and aligned with my highest self.
3. I create space for gratitude, replacing negativity with appreciation.
4. Each thought I choose builds the life I desire.
5. I celebrate every small step of progress on my journey to mastery.
6. Gratitude empowers my mind and opens the door to new possibilities.
7. My mind is a garden of positivity, and I nurture it daily.

Mind control is one of the most empowering skills you can develop. By mastering your thoughts, you become the creator of your reality rather than a passive participant in it. The strategies in this chapter are tools to help you harness the immense potential of your mind. Use them consistently, and you'll find that your thoughts become allies on your journey to peace, purpose, and transformation.

What Love Has to do With It

Love is one of the most transformative forces in existence. It transcends mere emotion, acting as a profound energy that can heal wounds, bridge divides, and elevate human consciousness. Far from being an abstract concept, love is a dynamic vibration that can be cultivated and amplified to impact every facet of our lives—from our relationship with ourselves to the way we interact with the world around us.

The Role of Love in Self-Growth

True transformation begins with self-love. Self-love is not self-indulgence or arrogance; it is the ability to view oneself with compassion, to embrace both strengths and imperfections, and to cultivate an inner dialogue that nurtures rather than criticizes. When you love yourself, you create a stable foundation for growth, becoming less reactive to external validation or criticism because your sense of worth arises from within. You don't need approval from others, because you approve of yourself.

Loving yourself means forgiving your mistakes and recognizing that you are a work in progress, we all are. For instance, if you fail to meet a professional goal, self-love enables you to reflect on the experience with curiosity rather than harsh judgment. This approach fosters resilience and encourages you to try again, viewing setbacks as opportunities for growth rather than reflections of your worth.

Many of us carry deeply ingrained beliefs that we are not enough. Self-love helps dismantle these limiting beliefs by replacing them with affirmations of our inherent worth. For example, someone who constantly doubts their abilities might begin practicing self-love by repeating affirmations such as, "I am capable, and I deserve to succeed." Over time, this practice shifts their internal narrative, creating space for new opportunities and possibilities.

When self-love is cultivated, it radiates outward, positively influencing all areas of life. For instance, a person who has developed self-love might naturally gravitate toward healthier relationships built on mutual respect and support. This inner foundation acts as a magnet for positive connections and experiences, transforming the way they navigate the world.

Love as a Connection to Others

Once self-love is established, it naturally extends outward. Love for others does not require perfection or the fulfillment of expectations. True love is a generous, unconditional energy that accepts people as they are while encouraging their growth into their best selves.

Love fosters empathy and understanding, enabling you to see the world through another person's eyes. For instance, when a friend is struggling, love allows you to approach their situation with compassion rather than judgment, strengthening your bond and offering them a sense of support. It also takes courage to love, as it often requires vulnerability. Sharing your true feelings with a partner, despite the risk of misunderstanding, deepens trust and creates a meaningful connection.

Love also has the remarkable power to heal and repair broken relationships. Through forgiveness and openness, it can dissolve resentment and rekindle connection. For example, a family conflict that has persisted for years may finally be resolved not through blame, but through acts of genuine care and understanding.

Love's capacity to connect, heal, and inspire is limitless. Practiced authentically, it builds bridges between people and enriches both their lives and the communities they form.

Universal Love: A Force for Unity

The ultimate evolution of love transcends the personal and becomes universal, rooted in the recognition that all beings are interconnected. Universal love shifts your perspective from separation to unity, transforming competition into collaboration and judgment into compassion. It allows us to see that the well-being of one is inseparable from the well-being of all.

Love also serves as a powerful protective force, shielding against lower vibrations like fear, anger, and hatred. Anchoring yourself in love cultivates inner peace and resilience, helping you remain immune to negativity even in challenging circumstances. For example, responding with understanding rather than frustration to hostility often disarms tension and fosters resolution.

Universal love inspires service and altruism, guiding actions that contribute to collective harmony and peace. Volunteering in your community, supporting those in need, or working toward a greater cause reflects this expansive, selfless love in action. By choosing love over division, we actively create a world that values collaboration and compassion over competition.

Practical Ways to Harness Love's Power

Love is not a passive feeling—it is an intentional practice. Begin with self-reflection and forgiveness. Reflect on areas where you may be holding onto pain or resentment, and actively practice self-forgiveness. For example, if you've been overly critical of yourself for a past mistake, write a letter forgiving yourself and acknowledging the lessons you've learned.

Affirmations of love can help reinforce the presence of love in your daily life. Repeat statements like, "I am surrounded and protected by love," or, "I radiate love to myself and others." These simple phrases align your thoughts with love's energy and create a positive internal dialogue.

Heart-centered meditation is another powerful practice. Visualize your heart as a glowing source of light, radiating warmth and compassion. Imagine this light expanding outward, first embracing yourself, then your loved ones, and finally extending to the entire world. This practice fosters inner peace and strengthens your connection to the collective.

Acts of kindness amplify love's energy. Small gestures, such as a thoughtful compliment or a helping hand, can create ripple effects of positivity. For example, taking a moment to express genuine appreciation to a colleague can uplift not only their day but also your own.

Esoterically speaking, the energy you give out will always return to you. If you find that others are being unkind or harsh toward you, it's worth taking a moment for self-reflection. Be honest with yourself about how you treat yourself and others—you may be surprised to discover that life often acts as a mirror, reflecting your actions and intentions back at you. This returned energy may not be immediate; it could take hours, days, weeks, or even months before it circles back.

This aligns with the timeless wisdom: **"What goes around comes around."** It also gives deeper meaning to the well-known teachings, **"Do unto others as you would have them do unto you"** and **"Love your neighbor as yourself."** When you view these statements not as preachings but as warnings, their significance becomes clear: love is not just a virtue, but a practical necessity. You get back what you give out.

So ask yourself: What kind of energy do you want to receive from others? Ponder this, and you'll begin to understand **what love truly has to do with it**.

Affirmations for Self-Love and Growth

1. I deeply and unconditionally love and accept myself as I am.
2. My imperfections are part of my unique beauty, and I embrace them with compassion.
3. I forgive myself for past mistakes and celebrate the growth they have inspired in me.
4. I am inherently worthy, and my value is not tied to external validation.
5. My confidence radiates positivity, attracting healthy relationships and opportunities into my life.
6. I am a work in progress, like everyone else, and every day I grow stronger and more resilient.

7. My inner dialogue is kind, supportive, and aligned with my highest good.

Affirmations for Love as a Connection to Others

1. I approach others with empathy, seeing the world through their eyes.
2. I give and receive love freely, unconditionally, and without judgment.
3. I am authentic and vulnerable in my relationships, fostering deeper connections.
4. Love flows from me to those around me, inspiring kindness and unity.
5. I forgive others and release resentment, creating space for harmony and peace.
6. My love inspires and uplifts those I encounter.
7. I celebrate the diversity in others and cherish the strength it brings to our connections.

Affirmations for Universal Love and Unity

1. Love is the energy that connects me to all living beings.
2. I choose love over fear, anchoring myself in positivity and strength.
3. My actions contribute to the harmony and peace of the collective.
4. I am part of a greater whole, and my love transcends boundaries of "me" and "them."
5. The higher vibration of love protects and uplifts my energy.
6. I see the divine in everyone and celebrate our interconnectedness.
7. Through love, I help create a world of unity, compassion, and joy.

Affirmations for Cultivating Love Daily

1. Gratitude opens my heart and allows love to flow abundantly in my life.
2. Every kind word and action I offer strengthens the energy of love in the world.
3. I visualize my heart radiating love to myself, others, and the entire planet.
4. Forgiveness releases my heart from burdens, freeing me to love unconditionally.
5. I am a source of love and light in the lives of those I encounter.
6. Each moment, I choose thoughts and actions that align with love.
7. Love is my guiding force, shaping a reality filled with meaning and connection.

These affirmations can be incorporated into your daily practice to reprogram your subconscious mind, fostering a life rooted in love, growth, and unity. Repeat each affirmation three times during your practice, and continue this routine consistently for at least 21 days to embed them into your subconscious.

Stop Trying and Start Doing

Reading this book may have sparked inspiration, hope, and a sense of clarity. You might have visualized the improvements you want to make in your life or how the principles shared here can transform your reality. That spark of insight is valuable, but it is only the beginning. The hard truth is this: inspiration alone is not enough to create meaningful improvements. Transformation happens only when action follows intention.

Many of us fall into the trap of "trying." Trying feels like movement, but in reality, it's a placeholder. It's an internal dialogue of "I'll start soon," or "I'm figuring it out," or "I'm working on it." Trying keeps you circling the edge of possibility without ever diving in. It feels safe because you're preparing, analyzing, or planning—but none of these activities generate tangible results.

True improvement begins when you stop trying and start doing. Doing is a state of commitment. It's taking that first step, however small, and then following through consistently. It's the recognition that progress is imperfect and sometimes messy, but it's still progress. Results, whether small or transformative, are a direct byproduct of consistent action.

Why "Trying" Holds You Back

The word "trying" often creates the illusion of effort without leading to meaningful movement or progress. When you tell yourself you're trying to change, you subconsciously leave space for excuses and hesitation. In essence, "trying" becomes a mental escape route, allowing you to avoid the discomfort of stepping into the unknown or committing fully to a goal. While it feels like you're taking action, it often keeps you stuck in a cycle of intention without follow-through.

For example, consider the statement, "I'm trying to meditate daily." In many cases, this might mean you're thinking about the benefits of meditation but haven't truly committed to integrating it as a consistent practice. Another example could be, "I'm trying to improve my health." Often, this masks hesitation to take small, actionable steps, such as committing to a daily 10-minute walk or making intentional, healthier food choices. Similarly, saying, "I'm trying to improve my mindset" might signify passively consuming motivational content without actually implementing the techniques that drive improvements.

The key issue with "trying" is that it implies a lack of full commitment. It signals hesitation and uncertainty, leaving you caught between intention and inaction. For example, when faced with a goal like starting a new workout routine, saying "I'm trying to exercise regularly" leaves room for excuses when challenges arise. However, replacing this with "I exercise regularly" demonstrates a commitment to take action, regardless of obstacles.

To move forward and create real improvement, replace "try" with "do." Instead of saying, "I'm trying to eat healthier," shift to "I am making healthier choices with every meal." This mindset fosters accountability and action, which are essential for progress. Similarly, instead of "I'm trying to focus more on gratitude," commit by saying, "I write three things I'm grateful for every day."

By committing fully and eliminating "trying" from your language, you transform vague intentions into decisive actions. This shift empowers you to move beyond hesitation and into a space of growth, accountability, and meaningful progress.

The Power of Doing

Doing requires courage. It means stepping out of your comfort zone and embracing the unknown. But doing is where the magic happens. It's the bridge between inspiration and reality, transforming dreams and ideas into tangible outcomes. This is where growth occurs—through action, results, and lessons learned along the way.

When you take action, you build momentum. That first step may feel daunting, but it sets a powerful chain reaction into motion. Momentum creates confidence. For instance, imagine you've always wanted to learn a new language but felt overwhelmed by where to start. By committing to just ten minutes a day with a language app, you soon find yourself picking up words, phrases, and the joy of progress. That small initial step snowballs into a steady journey of learning and confidence.

Clarity often emerges through doing. Many people delay action because they feel unsure about the next step or overwhelmed by the scope of their goals. However, clarity is rarely achieved by waiting for the perfect moment. Instead, it often comes from trying things, making adjustments, and discovering what works. Consider someone starting a new business. Their initial plan might be rough, but by launching and iterating based on customer feedback, they refine their offerings and align them with their vision.

Doing creates results, no matter how small. Each tangible action moves you closer to your goal. Even if the results are unexpected, they provide valuable lessons. For example, a person who commits to daily journaling for personal growth may find unexpected benefits—like reduced stress or improved creativity—beyond their original intent of organizing thoughts. Every effort counts, whether it's a direct success or an insightful misstep.

Taking action breaks the cycle of procrastination. Once you start, the inertia of inaction dissolves, and progress becomes possible. Imagine a student facing a massive assignment. The mere thought of starting might feel paralyzing, but simply sitting down and writing one sentence or organizing materials can shatter that resistance. That single step paves the way for sustained progress.

Examples in Everyday Life

A powerful example of "doing" is seen in fitness. Many people aspire to get healthier but struggle to begin. Someone might "try" to get fit by researching workout plans endlessly without ever stepping into a gym. In contrast, someone who decides to do just ten push-ups daily immediately begins building strength and forming a habit. Over time, the consistent doer achieves results that the perpetual planner never reaches.

Another example is in relationships. Instead of saying, "I'm trying to communicate better with my partner," the act of having one honest, heartfelt conversation marks the start of real improvement. Doing fosters connection and lays the foundation for improved dynamics.

Doing is a catalyst for growth, clarity, and transformation. It's about embracing imperfection and trusting that each step will guide you closer to your aspirations. By shifting from "trying" to "doing," you unlock the full potential of your efforts and discover the power of action in shaping your life.

How to Shift from Trying to Doing

Shifting from "trying" to "doing" is a transformative process that begins with taking small, intentional actions. Start small and simple by focusing on manageable steps rather than overwhelming tasks. For instance, if you're beginning a fitness routine, commit to a 10-minute walk instead of an intense workout. These small, consistent actions create a foundation for long-term progress.

Set clear intentions by replacing vague goals with actionable plans. Instead of saying, "I'll try to eat healthier," commit to "I will include one serving of vegetables with every meal." Specific goals provide clarity and direction, making it easier to transition from thought to action.

Embrace imperfection by letting go of the need for flawless execution. Perfectionism often paralyzes progress, but understanding that mistakes are part of the learning process allows you to take imperfect action with confidence. For example, a writer struggling to complete a novel might start by drafting a rough outline rather than waiting for the "perfect" idea to strike.

Create accountability to stay motivated and committed. Share your goals with a trusted friend (not with a crab in the bucket), join a group with similar objectives, or use tools to track your progress. For instance, if you aim to improve your mindfulness practice, consider joining a meditation group or using an app to log your daily sessions.

Focus on the present moment by narrowing your attention to the immediate next step. Instead of being overwhelmed by the entire project, ask yourself, "What's the one thing I can do right now?" This approach prevents procrastination and keeps you grounded in actionable progress.

Celebrate your wins, no matter how small. Acknowledging your achievements reinforces the habit of taking action and builds momentum. For example, if your goal is to save money, reward yourself by tracking milestones like saving your first $100. Recognizing progress reminds you that every step counts.

By integrating these practices, you can break free from the cycle of "trying" and step into the empowering reality of "doing," transforming your intentions into meaningful actions and results.

The Shift in Mindset: From "I'll Try" to "I Do"

The words we use profoundly shape our mindset and influence our actions. Saying, "I'll try," creates a mental loophole, leaving space for hesitation or excuses. Even "I will" suggests future intention, which can delay action. Instead, adopt the language of commitment by saying, "I do." This subtle but powerful shift creates a mindset rooted in action and immediacy.

For instance, instead of saying, "I'll try to wake up earlier," affirm, "I wake up at 6:30 a.m. each day." Similarly, instead of, "I'll try to start my project," commit with, "I dedicate 20 minutes to my project today." These statements remove doubt and ground you in the present moment of action.

This linguistic shift signals your mind to take action now, not at some vague point in the future. By stating "I do," you align your thoughts and behaviors with decisiveness, reinforcing your ability to take consistent, meaningful steps toward your goals. Over time, this practice builds discipline, confidence, and momentum.

A Call to Action

Right now, take a moment to reflect on something you've been "trying" to do. What is one concrete action—no matter how small—that you can take today to shift from intention to execution? Pause and write it down. This step may be as simple as sending an email, scheduling a task, or dedicating five minutes to focused work. Whatever it is, make a clear commitment to it and follow through without hesitation.

Transformation doesn't happen in the abstract; it happens in the doing. You don't need to have all the answers or a perfect plan to begin. What matters is taking that first step and building momentum. If your goal is to cultivate self-love, your action could be spending five minutes practicing affirmations or journaling about what you appreciate in yourself. If you want to master your mind, it might involve setting aside time for meditation or choosing to redirect a negative thought into an empowering one. If your focus is on creating meaningful relationships, your action could be reaching out to someone you care about or expressing gratitude to a loved one.

Think of the power of compounding actions. One small step leads to another, and over time, those steps create a path toward the life you envision. By consistently doing instead of "trying," you shift from inertia to momentum, from hesitation to confidence, and from possibility to reality.

Now is the time to stop trying and start doing. Write that action down. Commit to it fully. And most importantly, take the step. Each small victory strengthens your resolve and brings you closer to your goals. The results will follow, one step at a time, transforming your life in ways you never imagined.

Remember, as Yoda famously said in *Star Wars*: **"Do or do not. There is no try."** This is the true key to transformation. Success doesn't come from trying—it comes from doing. I know I've shared this quote earlier in the book, but it bears repeating because it is *that* important.

Affirmations for Courage and Commitment

1. I embrace action with courage, stepping out of my comfort zone to achieve my goals.
2. I do what needs to be done, knowing that growth comes from doing, not hesitating.
3. I face challenges head-on, transforming them into valuable opportunities for growth.
4. Each action I take brings me closer to the life I envision and deserve.
5. I trust in my ability to take the first step, even when it feels uncertain.
6. I allow courage to guide me, knowing that fear diminishes with every step forward.

7. My commitment to action fuels my confidence, resilience, and success.

Affirmations for Building Momentum

1. I create momentum by taking consistent steps toward my goals every single day.
2. Each action, no matter how small, propels me forward and strengthens my resolve.
3. I focus on progress over perfection, celebrating every small victory along the way.
4. With every step I take, my confidence grows, reinforcing my ability to succeed.
5. Momentum becomes my ally, making each new action feel easier and more natural.
6. I trust that consistent effort will transform my intentions into meaningful accomplishments.
7. I move forward with determination, knowing that momentum is the key to achieving my dreams.

Affirmations for Clarity Through Action

1. I discover clarity through doing, trusting that action will reveal the path ahead.
2. I take each step with curiosity, embracing the lessons and insights that come with experience.
3. Action opens doors to opportunities and solutions that were once hidden from view.
4. I trust the process, understanding that I don't need to have all the answers to begin.
5. Clarity grows as I engage with life, turning uncertainty into purposeful direction.
6. I release the need for perfection and welcome the discoveries that come through progress.
7. Each action I take strengthens my vision and aligns me with my goals.

Affirmations for Breaking Procrastination

1. I release procrastination and replace it with purposeful action that propels me forward.
2. I start exactly where I am, using the resources and strengths I already possess.
3. The first small step I take today dissolves resistance and unlocks powerful progress.
4. I act with intention, knowing that consistent effort builds the foundation for lasting success.
5. Procrastination no longer holds me back—I choose to be a doer, not a dreamer.
6. I approach my tasks with focus and determination, completing them one by one.
7. Each action I take reinforces my commitment to growth, productivity, and achievement.

Affirmations for Turning Dreams into Reality

1. I turn inspiration into reality by taking decisive and consistent action every day.
2. My dreams are worth pursuing, and I am fully committed to bringing them to life.
3. I trust in my ability to transform ideas into tangible outcomes through focused effort.
4. Each action I take is a declaration of my belief in my potential and my future.
5. I am the creator of my reality, shaping it intentionally with every choice I make.
6. I move forward with confidence, knowing that small actions lead to big results.
7. My dreams become my reality because I have the courage to act on them.

How to Use These Affirmations

Incorporate these affirmations into your daily routine by repeating each one three times with focus and intention. Pair them with moments of action to reinforce their power. For example, before beginning a task, affirm your commitment to doing and let the affirmation propel you forward. Over time, these affirmations will help reprogram your subconscious mind, making action a natural and consistent part of your journey.

Reading Is the First Step, Not the Destination

Reading is only the first step on a journey of transformation. Books, like this one, hold the power to inspire, educate, and reveal new possibilities. They are like maps, guiding us toward uncharted potential and offering perspectives we may never have considered before. Yet, while a map can show the way, it cannot take the steps for us. The act of reading, by itself, cannot bring about improvement. It is what we do with the knowledge we gain that shapes our reality.

Imagine someone who reads countless books on fitness and healthy living but never sets foot in a gym or improves their eating habits. The knowledge they've accumulated sits unused, a pile of unrealized potential. They may feel inspired by the vivid descriptions of transformation in these books, yet without action, their health remains unimproved. The spark of excitement they felt while reading fades, leaving them in the same place as before, yearning for improvement but unable to achieve it.

Inspiration alone is not enough. Feeling motivated is a beautiful thing—it ignites hope and fills us with the energy of possibility. But transformation requires more than a fleeting spark; it demands consistent action. Inspiration is the spark, transformation is the fire, and action is the fuel that keeps the flame alive. Without action, the ideas that once thrilled us become distant memories, and our dreams remain just that—dreams.

Consider another example: a person reads a book on improving relationships. They feel an emotional connection to the author's words and vow to communicate better with their loved ones. Yet, when faced with a real-life conflict, they fall back into old habits of avoidance or defensiveness. The ideas they admired in the book remain abstract concepts, and their relationships remain stuck in the same patterns.

But now, imagine what happens when someone takes action. A reader who internalizes what they've learned and commits to trying—whether it's having an honest conversation, taking small steps toward a healthier lifestyle, or practicing daily gratitude—sets a chain reaction into motion. Their actions, no matter how small, breathe life into the ideas they've encountered. The gym-goer who shows up for a 15-minute workout begins to feel stronger, both physically and mentally. The partner who practices active listening begins to see walls of misunderstanding crumble, replaced by deeper connections.

Books are powerful tools, but they are just that—tools. Their value lies in how we use them. Knowledge, when combined with effort, becomes the foundation for improvement. The first step is reading, but the destination lies in what we do next. Will you let inspiration fade, or will you let it drive you to action? The choice, and the transformation, are yours.

Knowledge Becomes Wisdom Through Action

Knowledge, no matter how profound or well-articulated, remains inert until it is applied. It is only through action that knowledge transforms into wisdom. Wisdom is not about acquiring endless information; it is about allowing what you know to shape how you live and how you engage with the world. The true power of knowledge lies in its application.

For instance, reading about mindfulness and its benefits will not bring you peace unless you take the time to practice it—whether through meditation, deep breathing, or simply being present in the moment. Similarly, understanding the principles of goal setting will not make your dreams a reality unless you take deliberate steps to implement a plan. Even when it comes to love, knowing how to cultivate deeper connections won't strengthen your relationships unless you choose to act with love, kindness, and vulnerability.

The gap between knowing and doing is where transformation happens. Every time you apply what you've learned, you bridge that gap and step closer to embodying the wisdom that knowledge can offer. Action breathes life into understanding, turning theoretical insights into meaningful improvement. Whether it's a small step or a bold leap, putting knowledge into action is the key to unlocking its true value and transforming your life.

Practice Is the Pathway to Transformation

Transformation doesn't occur through a single monumental leap; it unfolds through consistent, intentional practice. Each tool or concept you encounter—whether from a book, a mentor, or life itself—serves as a seed of potential. These seeds require care, effort, and persistence to bloom into meaningful improvements.

If you plant a seed in your backyard today, would you expect to see a tall, massive tree the very next morning? Of course not. Seeds need time to germinate, sprout, and grow into their full potential. Likewise, your journey of transformation requires patience, persistence, and decisive action. Trust the process, and in time, your tree of transformation will grow to astonish you.

Start by taking small, manageable steps each day. I have taught you about positive affirmations, commit to repeating them every morning, letting their power shape your mindset over time. I've helped you discover techniques for self-discipline, focus on applying them to one task daily, building your resilience gradually. I've taught you about improving relationships, begin with a single kind gesture or an open, honest conversation this week.

Every deliberate action, no matter how small, contributes to the momentum of improvement. Over time, these efforts compound, weaving together a pathway that leads to lasting transformation and growth. Remember, practice is not just repetition; it is the intentional, patient process of turning knowledge into wisdom and effort into excellence.

Dreams Don't Come True, Intentions Do

It's inspiring to imagine your goals and visualize a better version of yourself. The excitement of dreaming ignites hope, but dreams remain intangible without intention and commitment. Transformation requires action, even when the path is uncomfortable, inconvenient, or challenging. While this book may serve as your guide, the journey is yours to undertake, step by deliberate step.

Take a moment to reflect on what you've learned. Identify one lesson that resonated deeply with you, something that sparked a shift in your perspective or called you to action. Consider how you can apply that lesson today—not tomorrow, not next week, but now. Begin with small, consistent steps that turn inspiration into habit, weaving the lesson into the fabric of your daily life.

Dreams inspire, but intention and action turn them into reality. By committing to what you've learned and integrating it into your routine, you take ownership of your journey, ensuring that your aspirations are not just imagined but achieved.

Turning Reading into Results

Learning is most impactful when it transitions from theory to action. To truly benefit from what you've read, it's essential to take intentional steps to implement the lessons into your daily life. Knowledge, no matter how transformative, only becomes meaningful when applied.

Here's how you can turn the insights from this book into tangible results:

Start by **reviewing key takeaways**. Reflect on the ideas that stood out to you, the lessons that resonated deeply, or the concepts that sparked a sense of possibility. Write these down or highlight them as reminders of what you want to focus on. For example, if a section on mindfulness caught your attention, jot down specific practices, such as dedicating five minutes each morning to meditation.

Next, **create an action plan**. Break down the ideas you've identified into small, manageable steps. Decide how you'll incorporate them into your routine. For instance, if the book emphasized the power of gratitude, commit to writing down three things you're grateful for each evening. Small steps like these are achievable and, over time, create lasting habits that lead to meaningful improvement.

Hold yourself accountable by tracking your progress and seeking support. Write in a journal, set reminders, or share your goals with a trusted friend who can encourage you. However, be mindful of whom you confide in—avoid sharing with individuals who may discourage you, whether intentionally or not. These "crabs in a bucket" might downplay your efforts or project their fears onto your journey. Even well-meaning friends and family can sometimes undermine progress, so choose accountability partners who genuinely support your growth.

Revisit the book periodically. As you put its lessons into practice, your understanding will deepen, and new insights will emerge. Re-reading sections that were particularly impactful can reinforce your learning and provide fresh perspectives. For example, a chapter on **External Factors That Trigger Emotional Responses** might resonate differently after you've taken a few courageous steps toward your goals.

Example: Imagine you've read a chapter about **Reclaiming Your Power**. Initially, you decide to stop answering work emails after 8 p.m. and inform your colleagues of your new schedule. Over time, you notice the positive impact on your mental well-being. Revisiting the chapter later might inspire you to establish boundaries in other areas, such as saying "no" to social commitments that don't align with your values.

Turning reading into results is about aligning intention with action. By reviewing, planning, staying accountable, and revisiting what you've learned, you transform ideas into practices that enrich your life and move you closer to your goals.

A Reminder

The journey doesn't end when you finish this book—it begins. The power of transformation lies not in the pages of a book but in the hands of the reader. By turning what you've learned into action, you honor the knowledge you've gained and create a life that reflects your highest aspirations.

So, ask yourself: Will this book be another item checked off your reading list, or will it be the catalyst for meaningful improvement? The choice is yours. Start doing, and let the transformation begin.

Transforming Knowledge into Action

1. I take inspired action to bring my knowledge to life.
2. Every small step I take creates meaningful progress.
3. I turn lessons into habits and habits into transformation.
4. I honor what I've learned by applying it daily.
5. My actions align with the vision of my best self.
6. I am consistent in turning ideas into results.
7. Transformation begins with the choices I make today.

Fueling the Spark of Inspiration

1. The spark of inspiration within me grows into a steady flame.
2. I am motivated and committed to creating positive change.
3. Inspiration drives me, and action sustains my growth.
4. I welcome new opportunities to apply what I've learned.
5. Every day, I build momentum with intentional effort.
6. I turn fleeting inspiration into lasting transformation.
7. I am capable of achieving what I set my mind to.

Living in Alignment with My Goals

1. My actions are aligned with my deepest values.
2. I am focused on building the life I truly desire.
3. I release procrastination and act with clarity and purpose.
4. Every choice I make brings me closer to my goals.
5. I am disciplined and committed to my personal growth.
6. I have the power to create the reality I envision.
7. Each action I take is a reflection of my higher self.

Strengthening Relationships Through Action

1. I nurture my relationships with kindness and honesty.
2. I listen deeply and communicate with love and respect.
3. Each day, I show my appreciation for the people I care about.

4. I release defensiveness and choose connection instead.
5. I am open, vulnerable, and willing to grow with others.
6. I act with integrity and compassion in all my interactions.
7. My relationships thrive as I invest time and effort into them.

Building Confidence and Resilience

1. I have the courage to take bold steps toward my dreams.
2. I trust myself to handle challenges with grace and strength.
3. I am capable, resilient, and worthy of success.
4. With every action I take, my confidence grows.
5. I release fear and embrace opportunities for growth.
6. I focus on solutions and move forward with determination.
7. I am unstoppable when I commit to my goals.

How to Practice

Spend 10–15 minutes each day focusing on one set of affirmations. Repeat each affirmation three times before moving to the next, fully engaging your mind and emotions as you do so. Practicing consistently every day for 21 days allows these affirmations to take root in your subconscious mind. Rotate through all five sets over time to create a well-rounded and deeply ingrained sense of transformation.

The Illusion of "Trying"

The concept of "trying" is deceptively comforting. It gives the appearance of effort without requiring real commitment. When you say, "I'm trying to meditate" or "I'm trying to improve my habits," you often create a mental safety net—a way to excuse yourself from full accountability. While "trying" might seem like the beginning of progress, it frequently serves as a placeholder, a space where intentions linger without translating into tangible action. This illusion can trap you in a cycle of inaction, where the idea of improvement feels satisfying enough to delay the real work.

The Subtle Escape Route

"Trying" often becomes a psychological escape route. It allows you to tell yourself—and others—that you're working toward a goal without taking the vulnerable leap into execution. This mindset creates a limbo where you plan, analyze, and overthink but rarely act. It's easy to believe that contemplating improvement is progress, but transformation requires more than intention. For example, you might spend weeks researching the best meditation techniques without sitting down to meditate even once. While this feels productive, it keeps you distanced from the discomfort—and growth—that real action brings.

The Power of Commitment

True improvement begins with commitment. Doing, unlike trying, signals a willingness to act despite uncertainty, fear, or imperfection. It is a decision to engage fully with the process, understanding that success is built on consistent effort rather than flawless execution. For instance, instead of "trying to meditate," you commit to sitting quietly for five minutes each day, regardless of distractions or doubts. Similarly, rather than "trying to improve your mindset," you dedicate time daily to practicing affirmations or reframing negative thoughts. Commitment transforms vague intentions into concrete actions, paving the way for meaningful progress.

The Pen Analogy

A simple analogy illustrates this concept: Imagine a pen lying on a table. If someone asks you to pick it up, you either do it or you don't. There's no middle ground where you "try" to pick up the pen. Your hand either moves to grasp it, or it remains still. The same principle applies to the practices and techniques outlined in this book. Contemplating action won't yield results; only doing will. Every small step you take toward applying what you've learned bridges the gap between knowledge and transformation.

Results Are a Byproduct of Actions

Results are not achieved by sheer willpower, wishing, or even planning—they are the natural byproducts of consistent action. When you focus on taking steps rather than obsessing over the outcome, progress becomes inevitable. For instance, imagine someone who wants to lose weight. Instead of fixating on the scale, they commit to taking daily walks and eating balanced meals. Over time, the weight loss occurs naturally as a result of these actions.

Similarly, consider a writer working on their first book. If they dwell on the pressure of completing the entire manuscript, they may feel overwhelmed. However, by committing to writing just 500 words a day, they'll soon find their pages filling up. The final product is not the result of a single grand effort but the accumulation of small, consistent actions.

This principle applies to every area of life. Whether you aim to improve your relationships, build a new skill, or cultivate inner peace, results will follow when you prioritize doing. Each action you take creates a ripple effect, compounding over time to generate meaningful outcomes. Trust the process, and let the results take care of themselves.

Overcoming the Fear of Imperfection

One of the main reasons people remain stuck in the realm of "trying" is the fear of imperfection. The thought of making mistakes or falling short can be paralyzing. However, perfection isn't a prerequisite for growth— progress is. Embracing imperfection allows you to take action, learn, and adjust as needed. For example, someone hesitant to start writing because their first draft might be "bad" misses the point: the first draft is a necessary step toward improvement. By acting imperfectly, you create the opportunity for refinement and mastery.

Replacing "Trying" with "Doing"

To move beyond the illusion of trying, start by clarifying your intentions. Be specific about what you want to achieve and why it matters to you. Break your goals into small, actionable steps that you can tackle immediately. For instance, if your goal is to get healthier, commit to a 10-minute walk today rather than promising yourself you'll "start exercising soon." Fully commit to showing up every day, even if your efforts are imperfect. Let go of the need for immediate results and focus on the process. The act of doing itself is where transformation begins.

The Results of Action

The journey from where you are to where you want to be is bridged by action. Every time you shift from "trying" to "doing," you build momentum. Small, consistent steps compound over time, creating significant improvement. For example, someone who begins journaling daily for just five minutes might initially aim to organize their thoughts but soon discovers additional benefits like reduced stress and increased clarity. Each action, no matter how small, contributes to meaningful progress.

The choice is simple yet profound: Will you continue to "try," or will you commit to doing? The difference between the two is the difference between staying stuck and moving forward. Embrace the discomfort of doing, take that first step, and watch as momentum transforms intention into reality.

For example, a Navy pilot attempting to land his jet on an aircraft carrier may fail several times until he fully commits to the landing despite the challenges. In the middle of the open ocean, options are extremely limited. In such a scenario, my personal mantra—"Success is my only available option. Period."—takes on a real, profound, and even life-saving meaning.

Affirmations for Courage and Commitment

1. I embrace action with courage, knowing that growth begins outside my comfort zone.
2. I commit fully to my goals, taking deliberate steps toward their realization.
3. Each action I take is a declaration of my dedication and strength.
4. I act with purpose, transforming my intentions into reality every day.
5. I release hesitation and move forward with confidence and determination.
6. My courage inspires me to do what matters most, even when it feels challenging.
7. I honor my commitments to myself by showing up and doing the work.

Affirmations for Building Momentum

1. Each small action I take builds momentum toward my greater goals.
2. I celebrate progress over perfection, recognizing the value in every step forward.
3. I stay consistent, knowing that momentum creates powerful, lasting improvements.
4. My actions today pave the way for my success tomorrow.
5. Every effort I make strengthens my resolve and fuels my confidence.
6. I focus on doing, trusting that consistent actions lead to extraordinary results.
7. I build unstoppable momentum by taking one intentional step at a time.

Affirmations for Overcoming Fear and Doubt

1. I release fear and doubt by taking action, no matter how small.
2. I trust myself to figure things out as I go, knowing that doing creates clarity.
3. I act despite uncertainty, transforming fear into courage with each step.
4. My strength lies in doing what I can with what I have right now.
5. Every action I take replaces self-doubt with confidence and empowerment.
6. I move beyond hesitation, knowing that courage grows through doing.
7. I act boldly, choosing to focus on progress instead of perfection.

Affirmations for Results and Growth

1. I know that results are a byproduct of my consistent, focused actions.
2. Each step I take creates outcomes that align with my goals and aspirations.
3. I grow stronger and wiser with every action I take, no matter the result.
4. My actions lead to success, and every effort brings me closer to my dreams.
5. I embrace the lessons that come with doing, knowing they are key to growth.
6. I create tangible results by showing up and putting in the work every day.
7. I transform ideas into reality through decisive and committed action.

Affirmations for Clarity and Direction

1. I gain clarity through doing, letting each step reveal the path ahead.
2. I trust the process, knowing that action uncovers opportunities and solutions.
3. My commitment to action creates the direction I need to achieve my goals.
4. Each step I take aligns me with my purpose and strengthens my focus.
5. I trust that clarity grows as I move forward with intention and persistence.
6. I make decisions and act boldly, knowing that doing is the key to progress.
7. I turn uncertainty into certainty by taking consistent, meaningful action.

How to Practice

Spend 10–15 minutes each day focusing on one set of affirmations. Repeat each affirmation three times before moving to the next, fully engaging your mind and emotions as you do so. Practicing consistently every day for 21 days allows these affirmations to take root in your subconscious mind. Rotate through all five sets over time to create a well-rounded and deeply ingrained sense of transformation.

The Power of Decisive Action

The story of **Hanuman**, a beloved figure in Hindu mythology, is a profound lesson in faith, devotion, and decisive action. One particular tale from the *Ramayana* highlights his journey of self-realization and the power of committing fully to action when he embraces his potential.

Hanuman's Leap to Lanka: A Lesson in Decisive Action

In the epic *Ramayana*, Hanuman plays a pivotal role in the mission to rescue Sita, Lord Rama's wife, who has been abducted by the demon king Ravana. Sita is held captive in Lanka, a distant island surrounded by a vast ocean. At the shore, Rama and his allies, the Vanaras (monkey warriors), face the daunting challenge of crossing the ocean to locate Sita.

Though Hanuman is inherently divine and immensely powerful—being the son of the wind god Vayu and blessed with extraordinary strength—he had forgotten his abilities due to a curse. At this moment of uncertainty, Jambavan, the wise bear leader, reminds Hanuman of his immense potential. With this encouragement, Hanuman awakens to his true strength and resolves to act.

Without hesitation or overthinking, Hanuman takes a decisive leap across the vast ocean to Lanka. Along the way, he encounters obstacles, including the demoness Surasa and the mountain Mainaka, but overcomes them with clarity and focus. His unwavering determination ultimately leads to the discovery of Sita's location, a critical step in Rama's mission to defeat Ravana and restore harmony.

Hanuman's leap is a powerful symbol of courage, faith, and the transformative power of action. It demonstrates that even the most challenging tasks become possible when approached with conviction and purpose.

The Power of Decisive Action: Lessons from Hanuman

Decisive action is not just about movement—it is about purposeful and courageous effort that propels us toward our goals. Hanuman's leap exemplifies this principle and offers timeless lessons for navigating challenges in life.

Before the leap, Hanuman doubted his abilities, much like we often underestimate our own potential. Jambavan's reminder of Hanuman's innate strength mirrors the encouragement we sometimes need to unlock our confidence. Once Hanuman realized his power, hesitation dissolved, and he transformed doubt into determination.

This moment reminds us that belief in our abilities is not always necessary to take the first step toward action. What matters is realizing that, just as a raindrop is an inseparable part of the ocean, we are a spark of divinity. So take that step boldly and fearlessly, trusting in the hand of faith to guide you.

Standing at the edge of the ocean, Hanuman focused on his mission rather than the enormity of the task. He didn't let fear or analysis paralyze him. His singular focus on finding Sita and serving Rama gave him the clarity and courage to leap into the unknown. This teaches us that focusing on our purpose, rather than being consumed by potential obstacles, enables us to take decisive steps forward.

As Hanuman crossed the ocean, he faced numerous challenges. Each obstacle—whether it was Surasa attempting to block his path or Simhika trying to drag him down—tested his resolve. However, Hanuman approached these hurdles with adaptability and determination, staying focused on his goal. This highlights an important truth: challenges are inevitable, but with resilience and focus, they can be overcome.

Hanuman's successful leap and discovery of Sita were not just acts of physical strength—they were a testament to his faith, devotion, and commitment to his purpose. His actions remind us that true progress comes from taking bold, purposeful steps, even in the face of uncertainty.

Applying Hanuman's Wisdom to Daily Life

Hanuman's story is more than an inspiring tale; it's a guide for taking action in our own lives. It illustrates that recognizing our potential, focusing on purpose, and overcoming obstacles are key to achieving transformation.

To act decisively, start before you feel ready. Like Hanuman, don't wait for the perfect moment. Confidence often follows action, not the other way around. By taking even small steps, you begin to build momentum and discover your strength.

Focus on your purpose rather than perfection. Hanuman's unwavering focus on serving Rama allowed him to act without fear of failure. Similarly, when you focus on why you're taking action, it becomes easier to move forward despite doubts or challenges.

The ocean Hanuman crossed symbolizes the unknown—the vast, uncertain challenges we all face. Instead of letting fear hold you back, embrace it as a sign of growth. Courage isn't the absence of fear; it's the willingness to act despite it.

Obstacles are a natural part of any journey. Just as Hanuman faced challenges during his leap, you will encounter difficulties on your path. View them not as roadblocks, but as opportunities to learn, adapt, and grow stronger. Each challenge you overcome brings you closer to your goal.

Decisive action doesn't always mean taking a giant leap. Sometimes, it's about small, consistent steps—like practicing a daily habit, setting a boundary, or choosing a positive mindset. These incremental actions create lasting improvements over time.

The Lifetime Impact of Action

When you choose to act rather than hesitate, the results are transformative. Each step you take builds confidence, cultivates resilience, and fosters growth. Hanuman's leap shows us that action, driven by purpose and faith, has the power to overcome even the greatest challenges. The lessons from his journey encourage us to move beyond fear and hesitation and embrace the transformative potential of decisive action.

Take inspiration from Hanuman's leap and ask yourself: What is the first step you can take today toward your goal? Remember, transformation begins not in the planning, but in the doing. Just as Hanuman's leap bridged the ocean, your actions can bridge the gap between where you are and where you want to be. Trust in your purpose, take the leap, and watch as the impossible becomes possible.

Positive Self-Talk for Taking Decisive Action

Practice the following positive self-talk daily for **at least 21 days**, repeating each sentence **3 times** before moving to the next one. This repetition will help reprogram your subconscious mind and build habits of decisive action:

1. I trust myself to make the right decisions, even in uncertain circumstances.
2. Every step I take, no matter how small, brings me closer to my goals.
3. I have the courage to take action, knowing that growth comes from movement.
4. I release the need for perfection and embrace progress through consistent effort.
5. Obstacles are opportunities for growth, and I face them with determination.
6. I am capable, resilient, and fully equipped to handle any challenge that comes my way.
7. My actions align with my purpose, and I move forward with confidence and clarity.
8. I choose to act decisively, trusting that the path will reveal itself as I move forward.
9. I let go of doubt and replace it with faith in my abilities and intentions.
10. I am worthy of success, and my actions create the life I desire.

Repeat these affirmations daily, saying each one three times before moving on to the next. Practice this consistently for 21 days. As you speak each affirmation, focus on its meaning and allow yourself to feel the truth of the words. Visualize yourself embodying the decisive action you seek. This practice will strengthen your belief in your ability to take action and transform your mindset into one of empowerment and confidence.

Final Thoughts: Your Journey Begins Now

As you turn the last page of this book, remember: this is not the end—it is your beginning. What you hold in your hands is more than a collection of ideas; it is a guide, a call to action, and a toolkit for transformation. It is literally a "Human User Manual", your manual for improvement and transformation. But its power doesn't come from the words themselves; it comes from what you choose to do with them. Don't let this be just another book that sits on your shelf. Let it be the spark that ignites your journey, the companion that pushes you forward when you hesitate.

Transformation begins with a single step. Today, take that step—however small—and commit to it with your whole heart. Whether it's practicing one affirmation, setting aside five minutes for mindfulness, or reaching out to someone to strengthen a connection, action is what turns potential into reality. Tomorrow, take another step. Then another. With each action, no matter how simple, you move closer to the life you've envisioned. Momentum will build, confidence will grow, and the improvements you seek will begin to unfold.

The knowledge shared here is like a river—it flows endlessly with potential. I have led you to its edge, but only you can decide to drink. The power to transform your life has always been within you. This book has illuminated the path, but walking it is entirely up to you. The world doesn't improve through hesitation; it improves when you stop trying and start doing.

Your best life isn't just waiting—it's calling. So rise, act, and answer that call. Let today be the day you step into your power and claim the life you deserve.

Author of The Human User Manual: Unlock Your Potential, Master Your Mind, and Transform Your Life. Robert Ellis is passionate about personal growth, personal development and helping people achieve positive, lasting improvements in their lives.

www.ingramcontent.com/pod-product-compliance
Lightning Source LLC
Chambersburg PA
CBHW051512120626
46551CB00012B/883